A History
of Higher Education
in New Jersey

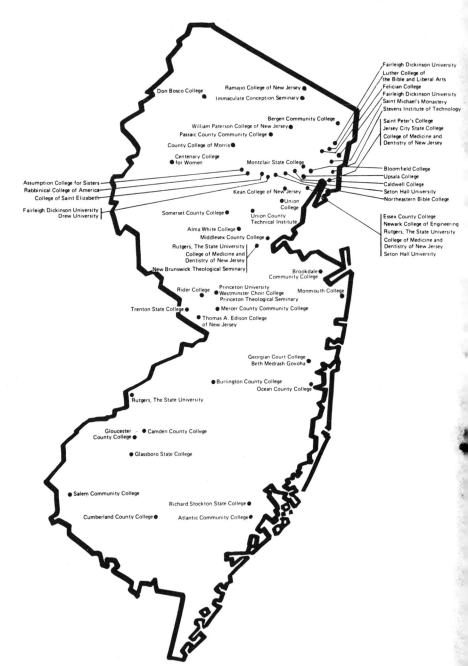

Fairleigh Dickinson University
Luther College of
the Bible and Liberal Arts
Felician College
Fairleigh Dickinson University
Saint Michael's Monastery
Stevens Institute of Technology

Saint Peter's College
Jersey City State College
College of Medicine and
Dentistry of New Jersey

Don Bosco College
Ramapo College of New Jersey ●
Immaculate Conception Seminary ●

Bergen Community College
William Paterson College of New Jersey ●
Passaic County Community College ●

County College of Morris ●

Centenary College
● for Women

Montclair State College

Bloomfield College
Upsala College
Caldwell College
Seton Hall University
Northeastern Bible College

Assumption College for Sisters
Rabbinical College of America
College of Saint Elizabeth

Kean College of New Jersey

● Union
College

Fairleigh Dickinson University
Drew University

Somerset County College ●

Union County
Technical Institute

Essex County College
Newark College of Engineering
Rutgers, The State University
College of Medicine and
Dentistry of New Jersey
Seton Hall University

Alma White College ●
Middlesex County College ●

Rutgers, The State University
College of Medicine and
Dentistry of New Jersey
New Brunswick Theological Seminary

Brookdale ●
Community College

Rider College ●
Princeton University
● Westminster Choir College
Princeton Theological Seminary

Monmouth College ●

Trenton State College ●
● Mercer County Community College

● Thomas A. Edison College
of New Jersey

Georgian Court College ●
Beth Medrash Govoha

● Burlington County College
Ocean County College ●

● Rutgers, The State University

Gloucester — ● Camden County College
County College ●

● Glassboro State College

● Salem Community College
Richard Stockton State College ●

Cumberland County College ●
Atlantic Community College ●

New Jersey's Colleges. BY PERMISSION OF THE BOARD OF HIGHER
EDUCATION, STATE OF NEW JERSEY

A History
of Higher Education
in New Jersey

Peter Sammartino
Chancellor, Fairleigh Dickinson University

South Brunswick and New York: A. S. Barnes and Company
London: Thomas Yoseloff Ltd

© 1978 by A. S. Barnes and Co., Inc.

A. S. Barnes and Co., Inc.
Cranbury, New Jersey 08512

Thomas Yoseloff Ltd
Magdalen House
136–148 Tooley Street
London SE1 2TT, England

Library of Congress Cataloging in Publication Data

Sammartino, Peter, 1904–
    A history of higher education in New Jersey.

    Bibliography: p.
    Includes index.
    1. Universities and colleges—New Jersey—History. I. Title.
LA331.5.S25   378.749   77-74110
ISBN 0-498-02095-9

PRINTED IN THE UNITED STATES OF AMERICA

to my wife, Sally

Contents

Preface

THIS WAS a difficult book to organize by chapters. With sixty institutions in the state, it was impossible to assign a chapter for each. Yet there are a number of colleges that are so old or so complex that a chapter for each one alone is justified. But no matter what basis was used, there were always some loose ends.

What does one stress in such a history—buildings, personalities, curricula? How does one avoid the aspect of a directory of colleges?

The format I have used is a mélange that gives major attention to the individual early colleges, brings out broad movements such as the state colleges and the community colleges, and, throughout, attempts to treat colleges and movements within the framework of New Jersey developments. Buildings are sometimes important because often they represent major changes in the development of a college. Personalities are sometimes important because they represent a major stamp on the college or university. Curricula are important when they indicate a major trend. Obviously, for the community colleges, it is more important to treat the broad movement as such, for the component colleges all moved together in a relatively short period of time.

Is the account too New Jersey-minded? I plead guilty. For too long a pejorative picture of New Jersey higher education has been painted. As I see the facts, over the decades New Jersey has been in the forefront. There were years of legislative procrastination as there are in every state, but on the whole, it has been a situation that must be equated with the size and shape of the state, with its proximity to two large bustling cities with population enclaves. The comparison, if one is to be made, is with Long Island or Westchester, both of whom, like New Jersey, are dependent areas of New York.

In a book of this sort, I tried to avoid indigestible statistics or eye-boggling references that make one lose the trend of thought. I hope the reader will go away with the story of the positive aspects of higher education in New Jersey.

I used four approaches. I read every book or thesis or account that I could find. I visited every college, and in most cases I spoke with a knowledgeable person at the institution either in situ or by telephone. In addition, I had a resource person at most, but not all, of the colleges. Usually, it was a person who had written or was writing historical material on the institution. Lastly, over the thirty years I have been involved with higher education in New Jersey, I have come to know certain key individuals each of whom has an overview of trends in New Jersey, and, with them, my discussions were more extended, even though in all cases they were also resource persons for individual colleges.

It has been an exhilarating experience, and the more I grew to know about each institution the more I appreciated its worth and its service to the state. I hope that others will restudy the course of higher education within the state and will write their accounts as they see it.

Acknowledgments

SALLY AND I enjoyed the visits throughout the state. She sometimes complained that too many books, catalogs, and articles were cluttering her office, but now they have been moved to the archives.

I wish to express thanks to my secretary, Mrs. Jeannette Schuffenhauer, for her patient deciphering of illegible manuscript, to Edith Heal Berrien for her editing, and to Mr. Clayton Hoagland for his chapter on Fairleigh Dickinson University.

Finally, my thanks to the following resource persons:

Dr. Merle F. Allshouse, Bloomfield College
Dr. Charles Angoff, Fairleigh Dickinson University
Dr. Richard E. Bjork, Stockton State College
Dr. Robert D. Bole, Glassboro State College
Dr. Clayton R. Brower, Trenton State College
Dr. Walter Brower, Rider College
Dean J. Douglas Brown, Princeton University
Dr. James D. Brown, Jr., Edison College
Father Clement Buckley, C.P., St. Michael's Monastery
Dr. Alvin R. Calman, Upsala College
Reverend Edward J. Ciuba, Immaculate Conception Seminary
Mrs. Mary H. Fairbanks, Department of Higher Education
Msgr. William Noé Field, Seton Hall University
Mrs. Marcy Goldstein, New Jersey Institute of Technology

Dr. Mason W. Gross, Rutgers University
Rabbi Moshe Herson, The Rabbinical College of America
Reverend Charles H. Immendorf, Luther College of the Bible and
    Liberal Arts
Very Reverend Francis J. Klander, Don Bosco College
Mr. J. Mark Lono, Drew University
Prof. James M. Lynch, Jr., Glassboro State College
Dr. Richard P. McCormick, Rutgers University
Sr. Blanche Marie McEniry, St. Elizabeth College
Dr. Kenneth C. McKay, Union College
Dr. William J. McKeefery, Paterson State College
Dr. William J. Maxwell, Jersey City State College
Dr. Albert E. Meder, Jr., Rutgers University
Dr. Gustavo Mellander, Passaic County Community College
Prof. James Pettigrove, Montclair State College
Mr. George Potter, Ramapo College of New Jersey
Prof. Donald R. Raichle, Kean College
Dr. Edward W. Seay, Centenary College for Women
Dr. Sidney Silverman, Bergen Community College
Dr. J. Harry Smith, Essex County College
Robert Van Benthuyser, Monmouth College
Rabbi Y. J. Weisberg, Beth Medrash Govoha
Dr. Kenneth E. Wright, Department of Higher Education
Reverend Victor R. Yanitelli, St. Peter's College

A History
of Higher Education
in New Jersey

1

Higher Education in New Jersey

ONE tends to think about higher education in terms of individual institutions, and indeed on the college level this approach was rational until the fourth or fifth decade of the present century. There were two movements within New Jersey that were state-propelled before this. The first was the result of the Morrill Act during the Civil War and, in New Jersey, occasioned the first step in the eventual development during the forties and fifties of Rutgers as a state university. The other movement that involved the state was the gradual evolution of teachers institutes into normal schools and finally into state colleges. One might add that during the thirties there was a state movement for the emergency two-year colleges, but this ended when federal funding ceased, although two private colleges were born from the ashes, Monmouth and Union, at which point direct state administration ended.

The next great statewide movement did not come about until 1962, when the community-college legislation was enacted. As a result about $220,000,000 has been spent in less than fifteen years for capital expenses. A further state development was the ascendancy of the newly-formed Board of Higher Education in 1967. While private institutions had been formerly free to add whatever courses they wished, now there was a growing limitation on courses and power that the Board assumed. The only private colleges not directly involved were Princeton, Stevens Institute of Technology, and Centenary College, all of which were formed before New Jersey had formally established a state charter. The Board controls the state institutions, which include the state university and the state colleges. While the community colleges are really creatures of the county, the state control is indeed very strong. But it also controls the private colleges, which at this point seem to exercise lesser influence since out of a board of eighteen members, only one is supposed to represent the twenty-nine private institutions within the state. The era of the public institutions had indeed become by the sixties and the seventies the dominant one.

Higher education in this country went through a difficult time during the thirties, and the record in New Jersey was no worse than in most of the states. During the war period, of course, almost everything was at a standstill. But during the fifties, in most states, things began to look up in higher education. Legislatures unloosed their purse strings and voters looked favorably upon bond issues for colleges. New Jersey was among those in the lead, and almost a half billion dollars was voted for new public college facilities.

New Jersey's Educational Facilities Act has made available in notes and bonds as of 1975, $366,332,000 for educational facilities for public and private colleges. Added to this is the amount allocated for new facilities by the federal 1963 education law, which up to 1975 had provided $33,177,701. This generated $100,000,000 worth of academic facilities. In addition, through the Housing and Urban Development Agency, $176,587,000 had been allocated for dormitories and other facilities. For a small state, it has been a tidy sum. But note that the numbers going out of state for their education had tended to change relatively little for reasons I shall explain.

True, New Jersey did not have a real state university until 1956, but even for this there is a good reason that I attempt to explain in the chapter on Rutgers. New Jersey was somewhat lethargic in embarking upon a community-college movement, but when it did, the state wound up with sixteen such colleges whose cost of $220,000,000 probably means that New Jersey is among the first five or six in the nation.

Note these other figures from the National Science Foundation Report on "Federal Support for Universities, Colleges and Selected nonprofit institutions." These include capital and research grants to New Jersey but exclude loans.

1963	$ 8,371,000
1964	9,687,000
1965	29,813,000
1966	29,224,000
1967	37,865,000
1968	29,999,000
1969	66,238,000
1970	26,849,000
1971	32,779,000
1972	45,448,000
1973	38,171,000
1974	49,546,000

Does the above give the impression of a lethargic state? Quite the contrary. It shows that both public and private institutions, in spite of large state allocations, were justifying federal grants—in most cases matching grants for capital and research purposes.

Observe the figures in another way. The following State of New Jersey appropriations for higher education include appropriations for general state operations, county colleges, and capital construction:

1967	$ 98,860,760
1968	107,391,311
1969	139,847,010
1970	154,471,077
1971	203,230,894
1972	248,767,486
1973	297,464,133
1974	334,876,865
1975	369,723,436
1976	348,746,468
1977	348,348,379

It can hardly be said that New Jersey is not doing its share in providing for higher education.

I would make this statement: for the young man or woman who wished to attend college during the twentieth century, the opportunities were above average in the northeastern part of New Jersey. And if the person could not attend during the daytime, there were opportunities in the evening. New Jersey did not equal the opportunities offered by the city colleges in New York City, but that system was sui generis and still is. Note, however, that their untrammeled growth has led to some very traumatic and bloodletting cuts.

After the war, there evolved a decided philosophy, not only in New Jersey but in most states, to think in terms of having the state provide a place for every student who wanted to go to college. There were movements, two federal and the other state, which tried to cater to both public and private institutions. The first was the Federal Higher Education Act of 1963, which allocated money to each state, which in time parceled it out to both public and private institutions, although when the act was first implemented in New Jersey, the public institutions refrained from submitting requests because of the state bond issues that were supplying their needs.

Until the sixties most private institutions had hesitated to erect new buildings until they had most or all of the money pledged or in hand. There was a tendency to shy away from mortgages, although these were necessary from time to time. But when the federal act was passed in 1963, it was an open invitation to all institutions, both public and private, to proceed on a debt basis. Institutions that had heretofore shrunk in horror of going into debt now changed their philosophy willingly, for two reasons. As a result of the depression of the thirties, and the war, and because of the rush for a college education, new facilities were badly needed. But the greater incentive was that under this law 33⅓% of the amount of the building was an outright grant, only 20% in cash was required, and the remaining 46⅔% was on a long-term, low-interest rate. Who could refuse such a deal? Even the well-heeled, astronomically endowed institutions that really had no need for such a handout couldn't resist the lure of using federal money and leaving their funds to draw much higher interest rates. The result was that in New Jersey, private colleges were able to construct within a short time much-needed buildings worth about $100,000,000, although this total reached $180,000,-000 because of certain aspects of the law. This move forward paralleled the effect of the state bond issue on the development of the public institutions. In passing, it is appropriate to mention the bond issues approved for public higher education:

1959	$ 66,800,000
1964	$ 41,000,000
1968	$202,500,000
1971	$155,000,000
Total	$465,300,000

More buildings were erected in a few years than had been erected since the beginning of higher education in the United States, and nowhere was the effect as electric as it was in New Jersey.

The other federal movement that added to facilities was the availability of loans for dormitories through the Federal Housing and Urban Development Agency, and this also added to the patrimony of the state.

The state movement that was to fill the gap in case public and private institutions had not completely filled their requirements, was the New Jersey Educational Facilities Authority originally created in 1966. Under this plan both public and independent colleges can borrow money through the sale of tax-exempt notes and bonds as arranged by the Authority. All sorts of facilities are covered: dormitories, classroom and laboratory buildings, libraries, student unions, health and athletic facilities, research buildings, even parking areas. In fact, loans can be effected even for the purchase of existing buildings that may be near the college campus and that could contribute to its academic program. The implementation of the act was held up pending court tests, especially in regard to church-related colleges. Loans, however, could not be used for the training of church personnel or for the teaching of a particular religion. This proviso, which is a part of all federal programs as well, in no small way contributes to the growing secularization of church-related colleges.

The great advantage, of course, is that because of the tax-exempt character of the bonds, it means that institutions can borrow money more cheaply than through ordinary commercial means. By the end of 1975, over $336,332,000 in bonds and notes covering sixteen institutional projects had been approved. Another major step forward! The net result of all these programs is that New Jersey has more than enough facilities to take care of all its needs, even though, here and there, there may be a few minor needs in both public and private colleges.

What happened after the war was that everybody learned how to borrow money—the federal government, the states, and the municipalities. And, if one couldn't do it directly, then one formed a special authority to create tax-free bond issues, and there were always plenty of investors around who would buy these bonds. It opened a new era for many institutions, and certainly for colleges and universities. Whereas in the past colleges looked upon borrowing with trepidation, in the fifties, the idea of "build now—pay later" took hold. Today most colleges, unless they are heavily church-related, owe money to the Housing and Urban Development agency for dormitories, to the federal government for educational buildings under the 1963 Higher Education Act, to the state for special bond issues, and to a higher education facilities authority for a wide variety of buildings. One might say that the installments to be paid are really a part of operational costs and should be figured in these costs as they are reflected in student tuition.

Curiously, there has been over the last few decades a canard that in higher education New Jersey was at the bottom of the barrel—a canard based on a meaningless statistic issued by the Department of Health, Education and Welfare. The listing takes the amount spent on public higher education divided by population and rates the states accordingly. At the present time probably 45% (although there are no up-do-date figures) of full-time New Jersey students are enrolled in out-of-state colleges. Naturally, if one takes the total population and divides it by the expenditures for public higher education, one gets a low statistic. But it is a meaningless statistic, just as meaningless as the fact that New Jersey is the forty-fifth state in terms of size. But if one takes the average spent per student in public institutions, New Jersey is among the first in the country.

One may then ask why do half go out of the state? For
two very good reasons: one, the populated parts of the state,
the northeastern sector and the Camden sector, are both
parts of the New York and Philadelphia metropolitan area,
respectively, and as long as transportation holds up, there
will always be a natural inclination for some students to step
over the mythical state line and commute to an out-of-state
college, just as there are New York and Pennsylvania students who now commute to New Jersey. Second, New Jersey
being a relatively rich state, there will always be many students who will want to go to college away from home. Now,
if a student goes 150 miles north, east or west, New Jersey
being so small, he will be out of the state. New York State
in its Eccles report found that no matter how much it spent,
the same proportion went out of state. In New Jersey the
same thing has happened. In spite of capital expenditures of
about a billion dollars for public and private institutions, the
percentage going out of state has decreased from 54% in
1968 to probably about 45% in 1975. But the decrease has
been mainly due to another factor, the growth of the community colleges that have been attracting young people who
heretofore had not been going to college, including many
blacks and Puerto Ricans.

There is a great deal of seesawing from year to year with
regard to the relative position of the states in the national
picture on higher education, and slightly different premises
may give unusual results. For instance, in the year 1973-74,
New York was second in state appropriations for higher
education, but for the percent of change over a two-year
period, it ranked twenty-fifth. That 1973-74 period New
Jersey ranked eleventh in appropriations and seventh in
percentage of change over a two-year period. If one takes
the amount of money spent per student in public institutions,
New Jersey ranks fourth or sixth depending on slightly
different methods of computation. But generally speaking,

I believe that it would be correct to say that New Jersey certainly has been among the first ten states by any form of realistic computation one can devise over the decades. The true story of New Jersey is that most of the time it has been in the vanguard if one considers movements over a decade. A better comparison could be made with Long Island—all of it—both New York City and beyond. Both were agricultural hinterlands of New York City, which as a chief commercial center established operas, symphony, theaters, and colleges first. Later, when the population filled in the farmland, colleges filled in.

But even in colonial times when Massachusetts, Connecticut, New York, Pennsylvania, and Virginia had one college each, New Jersey had two—College of New Jersey (Princeton) and Queen's (Rutgers). In teacher education, New Jersey started in the teacher institutes in 1856. Today, the evolution from teachers colleges to state colleges has been nothing short of dramatic in New Jersey. In community colleges, New Jersey came a little later, but note that with a population of 7,330,000 it has sixteen such colleges compared with 7 in New York City with a population of 7,895,000. All of the New Jersey community colleges have outstanding campuses; all are doing an above-average job nationally.

Yes, in some areas of graduate work New Jersey is behind simply because New York City and, to a lesser extent, Philadelphia had begun in that area first. This state did not have a medical school; now it has two. New Jersey still has to catch up in some doctoral areas, but it's difficult to do so when out-of-state universities have evolved first. The development of private colleges, whether church related like Seton Hall or nonsectarian like Fairleigh Dickinson University, has been vigorous indeed.

In engineering, the role of Princeton, Rutgers, Stevens Institute, the New Jersey Institute of Technology, and Fairleigh Dickinson has been noteworthy in meeting local and national needs.

Even during the depression when everything was at a standstill, New Jersey took the lead in establishing six emergency colleges. During the war, of course, nothing could be done, but during the fifties and sixties, New Jersey pursued an all-encompassing course second to none.

True, for decades there was an ambivalence regarding our state university. In 1865 Rutgers had been designated as the land-grant institution in the state. For many decades there was indecision as to whether it should retain its private character or swing entirely into a state university, but after the war the latter course was taken, and since then it has become a great state university.

Some idea of the development of Rutgers, the State University may be gained by comparing the state budget for the State University in 1925, which was $1,138,172, with the budget fifty years later, which was $178,559,811. The total investment in plant as of June 30, 1945, was $20,193,889. On June 30, 1975, it was $335,257,093.

One aspect not often mentioned is that the student who has to work has above-average possibilities for evening liberal arts and career courses all over the state. And, if he wants an external degree, there is Edison College to serve him—a college in the vanguard.

Even in the sparsely settled areas of South Jersey, there is a new college—Stockton, plus seven community colleges, plus Glassboro State College, plus a campus of the State University at Camden. Compared with the population, the eight southern counties have more college places than probably any other similar area in the country.

Yes, New Jersey has it all—or almost all. It has no veterinary, osteopathic, chiropractic, or podiatry school, but it has a School for Advanced Studies and Westminster

Choir College. Going back to the comparison with Long Island (and I don't mean this in disparagement), it should be apparent that through the centuries and during the last few decades, New Jersey has been ready to meet its needs and that both private and public colleges and universities have been forging ahead bravely and enthusiastically.

2

Princeton University

TO UNDERSTAND Princeton, one needs to have an overall view of colonial colleges. All were an outgrowth of the
English desire for an educated people and a learned clergy.
Their origins were marked by the influence of religious
sects as were Harvard, founded in 1636, Yale, founded in
1701, and the College of William and Mary, established in
1693.

When Princeton was granted a charter as the College of
New Jersey by the royal governor, John Hamilton, on
November 22, 1746, it was the only college between New
Haven and Williamsburg. It was to be a college in the
tradition of Presbyterianism adhering to the principles of
Calvin, established by the immigrants from Scotland and
Ulster who had brought the Presbyterian faith with them.
It is interesting to note what a strong hold the clergy held
over the years. Every president of Princeton down to 1902
was a clergyman.

During the last week of May 1747, eight or ten students
assembled at the home of Jonathan Dickinson, the first
president of the college and the acknowledged leader of the

Presbyterian synod of New York. The students slept in spare bedrooms of the house. Dickinson's library was at their disposal.

The start was promising, but unfortunately, Jonathan Dickinson died four and a half months later. Aaron Burr, the father of the future vice-president of United States, was elected the new president. The students packed their trunks and rode six miles to the home of Aaron Burr, in Newark. The new governor of New Jersey, Jonathan Belcher, issued a new charter because of the attacks of the Anglicans who questioned the validity of the old one. Aaron Burr was officially and unanimously named the new president under the new charter on November 9, 1748, as voted by the trustees.

It was a humble second beginning. Some of the students roomed and boarded with the president. Others lived in outside homes. There was a lack of lecture halls, of a library, and of scientific equipment. Above all, there was a lack of money. The president served three years without pay. A few gifts came along, and by 1754 they amounted to £1,800 in New Jersey currency. A lottery was launched and 8,000 tickets were printed by Benjamin Franklin and distributed principally in Philadelphia, New York, Boston, and Virginia. Curiously, tickets could not be sold in New Jersey. Later, another lottery was launched in Connecticut. The returns were meager, and finally it was decided that the Reverend Gilbert Tennent and the Reverend Samuel Davies voyage to England to raise funds for the college. They succeeded in raising £1,700 and £500 more in Scotland. In view of the successful fund-raising efforts, it was decided to erect a college building. The question was, where to find the site. New Brunswick was considered, but it could not meet the trustees' requirement of a thousand pounds in New Jersey currency plus ten acres for a campus and two hundred acres of woodland for fuel. Then the village of Princeton met all the requirements, and the college was established there. The building that was eventually erected was named Nassau Hall in honor of the illustrious family of King William III. The move to Princeton was made in November of 1756, and it was here that the College of New Jersey was to maintain for more than a century its reputation as the religious and educational capital of Presbyterian America, providing the intellectual leadership for educating young men for the ministry.

In 1767, failing to find a religious leader of their own persuasion, the trustees elected Dr. John Witherspoon, a distinguished scholar and church leader of Scotland, for president. At that time the college was facing a tenuous existence, and by 1769 total assets amounted to only £2,535. Dr. Witherspoon, whose term of office ran from 1767 to 1795, was one of the great presidents of the college and a good fund raiser. He traveled throughout New Jersey, Pennsylvania, Maryland, Virginia, and South Carolina, raising £1,451 for the college. By 1760 the library contained 1,281 books and the first catalogue was completed.

As the states approached the great conflict for freedom, the students were caught up in a flurry of patriotic enthusiasm. Dr. Witherspoon was a member of the Somerset Committee of Correspondence, a leader in the move to imprison the royal governor, William Franklin, and not much later was urging the passing of the Declaration of Independence at the Continental Congress. The single building of the college was in turn occupied both by English and by Continental troops. It was a dreary period indeed, and in 1777 and 1779 Nassau Hall was used as a military hospital.

By 1779 the financial situation deteriorated even further due to the depreciation of currency. Dr. Witherspoon and Joseph Reed embarked for England to raise funds for the

College. The time was hardly propitious for collecting contributions for the unruly colony.

But while the college suffered financially, it gained in prestige. At the 1783 commencement—which was attended by General Washington—seven signers of the Declaration, nine signers of the Articles of Confederation, eleven future signers of the Constitution, and many members of Congress made up the illustrious company.

In 1793 there was talk of a union with Queen's College in New Brunswick, now Rutgers. Both institutions were in financial difficulties, but nothing became of the suggested merger.

In the meantime, the character of the college was changing. There was no longer a majority of the graduates preparing to enter the ministry. It was, by the time Dr. Witherspoon left, a place where practically all the students were preparing for public life. It should be borne in mind that in the absence of secondary schools, the students entering college during the eighteenth century were generally of a younger age.

In 1795 Dr. Witherspoon's very able son-in-law, Dr. Samuel Stanhope Smith, succeeded him as president. The financial situation was so bad that an appeal for funds was made to the state of New Jersey. The appeal was turned down because the college was by tradition controlled by one denomination. But on the promise of liberalization, $4,800 was voted to the college for repairs and the purchase of books and scientific equipment. In accordance with the spirit of the grant, the next two vacancies on the Board of Trustees were filled by Episcopalians. But the public reaction to the grant was unfavorable, and this avenue of help was closed for the future. It may seem a small matter retrospectively, but it was the sort of reaction that forced an adherence to the private character of the institution and eventually made it one of the great institutions of the world.

The enrichment of the meager science laboratory was pursued almost from the beginnings at Princeton, and in 1771 Dr. Witherspoon purchased an orrery from Dr. Rittenhouse for £416, a large sum in those days. Science and mathematics were vying for a place in the college curriculum, and slowly a full curricula in sciences and engineering burgeoned in a later century.

In 1802 tragedy struck when Nassau Hall was destroyed by fire. Some people blamed it on a group of students infected with Jacobin ideas, but the charge was never proved. The trustees immediately embarked on a fund-raising campaign, and in the end the tragedy had a rejuvenating effect on the institution. Nassau Hall was rebuilt, and as time went on the public came to know the college better.

In the beginning, athletic sport was looked down upon as frivolous, but student-directed activities were gradually expanded and in the end became more popular and more prestigious than the two literary societies, Whig and Clio. These debating and philosophic groups had built their own halls and enriched the intellectual life of those who belonged.

But the greatest change taking place was in the religious orientation of the college. Fewer and fewer theology students were registering, and undoubtedly the lack of money had a great deal to do with it. The college was becoming a place where people with money could send their sons to prepare for law and for business. Even though the need for Presbyterian ministers in the growing country was greater than ever, there was a mere trickle of candidates for the ministry each year, and most, if not all, were scholarship students. There was a move to establish a divinity school within the college, but in the end the decision was to found a seminary in the town of Princeton that became l'enfant chéri of the Presbyterian Church. The College of New Jersey, while still holding on to the apron strings of the

Church, became predominantly an arts college. The seminary students, all three of them, lived first at Nassau Hall, but in 1815 moved when the seminary owned its own hall. However, the Presbyterian Church, through the trustees, still controlled the College of New Jersey.

One must remember that the students were three or four years younger than the students of today. Their deportment in the early decades of the nineteenth century was fractious, to put it mildly. Explosion of gunpowder, the ringing of the college bell at three in the morning, the cutting through of the chapel Bible to insert a pack of playing cards, the shuffling of feet in the dining room—all added to the problems of the distraught administration and tutors.

Commencements were held late in September, necessitating attendance through the hot summer months. Beginning in 1844 it was decided to hold commencement on the last Wednesday in June, followed by a summer vacation of six weeks; then a nineteen-week term, a winter vacation, and a second term of twenty-one weeks. Thus began the pattern that holds true in most colleges today, except that the summer period has lengthened to almost three months and the terms shortened to fourteen or fifteen weeks.

As the generations rolled by, a number of factors began to change the character of the college, and this was true of other colleges in the country as well. The division between the seminary and the arts college deepened. As the financial support by the Church grew less, the contributions of alumni increased and the nontheological subjects such as mathematics, physics, astronomy, and modern languages were emphasized.

When the Civil War broke out, the Southern students left almost en masse, most of them to serve the South. It was an unhappy parting of the ways as fellow undergraduates clasped hands, each one to fight for his own side. Once again the college faced a difficult period, but the role of the alumni now overrode any calamities that could befall it. The alumni included some of the outstanding leaders of the country. For instance, former President James Madison became president of the alumni association and even left a modest contribution to Princeton in his will. The enrollment had been moving up, too. In 1829 it was 150; in 1847 it was 270.

There were new buildings: dormitories, East and West Halls, Stanhope Hall, Philosophical Building, and later, a small gymnasium. In the shuffle, architectural unity was lost as it was in other campuses. It wasn't until State bond issues made instant mammoth campus layouts, adhering to a harmonious architectural plan, that unity was achieved in American higher education. The Princeton library, completed in 1860, open two days a week, was really a storeroom since there were no student desks.

Fraternities were introduced in 1843, but by 1864 there were supposed to be no secret societies at Princeton. However, eating clubs had been forming as early as 1846. Thus there was at this early date the problem that has plagued all colleges, for the dining-hall food was usually mediocre and the students were driven to other means of procuring meals. In the process, boarding-house groups often led to the formation of fraternities. But at the College of New Jersey there was an alternate answer. The eating club, which omitted the secret aspect of fraternities, developed and was thus able to receive administrative sanction.

Under the administration of President John MacLean (1853-68) the college was able to acquire an adequate endowment and, by establishing a number of scholarships, was able to start Princeton on the path of selectivity. At the end of the Civil War all the members of the faculty were still Presbyterians and most of them ministers. But a change had come in the provenance of students. Before the war many came from the Southern planter states—Virginia, South

Carolina, Tennessee, and Kentucky. After the Civil War they came mostly from New Jersey, Pennsylvania, and New York.

The Reverend James McCosh, the second president to be brought over from Scotland, was president from 1868 to 1887. To him belongs the credit for bringing Princeton up to university standards. He introduced the best of European systems and insisted on scholarly attainment. He also changed the method of instruction from emphasis on drab repetition of outmoded material to the more relevant needs of a growing nation, and he achieved this by offering a superstructure of electives. Donations of $3,000,000 during his administration, indicative of the growing wealth of American leaders, enabled the institution to rise to a new level of physical splendor, including a better library, the second best in the country, and the addition of more scientific equipment. Postgraduate courses were developed, and a department of engineering was established that was later to blossom forth into a School of Engineering.

Since the students heretofore had been roughly fourteen to eighteen years of age, and since standards were getting higher, the college felt that it was time to introduce a preparatory school. The same movement was seen to be taking place elsewhere. The preparatory school at Princeton became the Lawrenceville School, with a fine reputation to this very day.

Sports continued to increase in importance, and on November 6, 1869, the first football match took place with Rutgers, which scored six goals to Princeton's four. Hereafter the campus heroes were no longer the gifted debaters of Whig and Clio, but the best football or baseball players.

The proportion of wealthy students was increasing steadily, and, to the horror of the trustees, in 1879 it was found that one third of the students were Episcopalians. The number of religious students was minimal. It was therefore decided to build Edwards Hall where good students of Presbyterian faith and little money could reside at low cost.

As McCosh retired in 1887, he proposed to the trustees that the institution be designated a university since it had all the elements of one, even though lacking a school of medicine and one of law. To his sorrow, the new designation was not to come until 1896 when, at the sesquicentennial celebration, it was declared that the title of the institution would be Princeton University. The idea of a Graduate College also came into being.

In 1901 the Graduate Department was henceforth known as the Graduate College, with Professor Andrew Fleming West as the first dean. This was a most important development.

Francis Landey Patton succeeded Dr. McCosh as president and served until 1902. By the turn of the century Princeton had more than 1,200 students, and this was a measure of the importance of the school. In 1893 the honor system for the conduct of examinations was instituted. The system has, since then, been successfully administered *by* the students.

Woodrow Wilson was elected president in 1902. Although he served only eight years, his influence was to last far beyond his term. For the proliferation of courses that had developed under the free elective system, he substituted a more limited arrangement of courses, including significant subjects within the departments of concentration. Admission standards were tightened. In 1905 he instituted the preceptorial system of instruction and brought in fifty young men as precepts. He believed in the integration of both the undergraduate and graduate segments, and in this he differed with Dean West, who secured a seeming victory by having the contributions for a new graduate building limited to an off-campus area.

Dr. John Grier Hibben succeeded Wilson, who had

decided to enter politics and was elected governor of the state. Endowments had increased five-fold, and the enrollment had now reached 2,400. The trustees decided in 1923 that enrollment would be limited. This, too, was to be a pivotal decision in the history of Princeton. The School of Architecture was established in 1919. Two years later the studies in engineering were re-formed as a School of Engineering. In 1930 the School of Public and International Affairs was established as an interdepartment development.

In 1923 a new system of reducing the subjects in the last two undergraduate years in order to provide for independent work on a thesis was initiated.

President Harold Willis Dodds was elected president in 1933. He faced the chaotic period of a depression and a World War, but Princeton stood firm throughout, principally because an energetic and generous alumni stood by. The world-famous Harvey S. Firestone Memorial Library was opened in 1948. The School of Public and International Affairs was renamed in honor of Woodrow Wilson as it moved to its striking new building in 1952.

In 1957 Dr. Dodds was succeeded by Dr. Robert Francis Goheen, and, as in many universities, changes took place. To the horror of many alumni, women were admitted for degree work in 1969. There was a specific program for the enrollment of disadvantaged minorities. The undergraduate enrollment expanded to 4,000. Interdepartmental programs were developed and a greater dedication to public and community problems was indicated in both engineering and architecture.

One of the greatest changes was the enormous increase in endowment and other funds. Indeed, if one analyzes all gifts added to its assets, Princeton had probably approached the "billion dollar club" where Harvard and Yale were already members.

President Goheen was succeeded in 1967 by William

Gordon Bowen. In this small volume I shall leave the history of incumbent presidents to future writers, but it would not be amiss to say that President Bowen has already sought to solidify the financial basis of Princeton, to push ahead the integrated character of undergraduate and graduate studies, and to strengthen the future development of the university.

3
Rutgers, the State University

FEW INSTITUTIONS have had to contend with as many problems as Rutgers, and it is a good example of how a church-related college eventually becomes a nonsectarian state university. Founded by the Dutch Reformed Church as Queen's College in honor of Queen Charlotte of the Netherlands, it might be said that in a sense it was a national college, representing one segment of the Dutch Church in America. Governor William Franklin granted the petitioning group a charter on November 10, 1766. The charter provided for forty-one trustees and included the governor—president of the Council—the chief justice, and the attorney-general of New Jersey, all ex officio, also six ministers and eight laymen from New Jersey, five ministers and sixteen laymen from New York, and two ministers from Pennsylvania. All but a few of the laymen were members of the Dutch Church.

The college was not to be exclusively concerned with the training of ministers, but with that which was stated at the first commencement: "The improving of the human mind, for the proper discharge of our Several Duties towards God, ourselves and our Neighbors."

The first president, Jacob Rutsen Hardenbergh, whose mother tongue was Dutch, apologized in public for his poor English. The Dutch wanted a college of their own, but their constituency was relatively a small one, and this was to provide difficulties for many years to come.

Because of the discord within the Dutch Church itself and because of certain objectionable features in the charter, Governor Franklin issued a new charter on March 20, 1770. This charter emphasized the need for the training of an able and learned ministry. The president was to be a member of the Dutch Church and a professor of divinity.

While the original charter was issued in 1766, it wasn't until May 7, 1771, that at a meeting in Hackensack it was decided by a vote of ten to seven to establish the college at New Brunswick rather than Hackensack. The college opened in 1771 using the building of the Red Lion Inn. The single tutor was Frederick Frelinghuysen, eighteen years old and a graduate of Princeton. There was a mere handful of students, but sharing the facilities were the more numerous students of the Grammar School. It is well to repeat that there were extremely few secondary schools at this time in the United States. College students might be anywhere from fourteen to nineteen years old, and came to college directly from a grammar school or a private tutorial arrangement. Because Frelinghuysen and a later tutor, John Taylor, were both graduates of Princeton, the curriculum was naturally patterned after that of the College of New Jersey. In the lower classes there was the study of Latin, Greek, arithmetic, and geometry. In the upper classes, geography, natural philosophy, mathematics, logic, and grammar were scheduled. As at Princeton, a debating and literary society was formed, the Athemar Society. It was this extracurricular activity that added immeasurably to the education of the students.

The college had hardly begun when it was caught up in

the Revolutionary struggle. Most of the few students enlisted. Twice the college was suspended but John Taylor, with a half dozen students, resumed classes late in 1777 in North Branch, and later in Millstone, both small hamlets not far from New Brunswick. Finally, in May of 1781, the college was able to reopen in New Brunswick, but conditions were hardly pleasant for the institution. There was little money; in 1782, there were still only eighteen students. There was no president (indeed there were no presidents for the first ten years), and the tutor's salary was in arrears. In 1784, the college seems to have vanished although the Grammar School continued in operation.

But somehow things brightened when the first president, Dr. Jacob Rutsen Hardenbergh arrived in 1786. As far back as October 12, 1774, the Reverend Hardenbergh had been selected by the Trustees as the speaker for the first commencement. John Taylor resumed his job as tutor, and a new two-story building was erected the following year. In 1793, a trustee committee met with a Princeton committee to discuss the possibility of merging the two schools by maintaining a preparatory school in New Brunswick and a college in Princeton. The plan was turned down by the Queen's trustees by a vote of nine to eight. But the relations with the Church were very tenuous and with no money forthcoming, Queen's was again suspended in 1795. Suddenly the college was revived in 1809 or thereabouts, the change occurring because of the interest of local citizens of New Brunswick. But this renewal of interest was complicated by the fact that the Church was less interested in the college than in the seminary that was a part of the college. The Church was willing to pay for the seminary professor and half the cost of a new building, known today as Old Queen's. The building was completed in 1811 and was to house the Grammar School, the College, and the Theological Seminary, but it provided no living quarters for students.

It is to be noted that the new student literary society, Calleopean, had accumulated a library of 200 books, and it was the extracurricular activity of this society that was a balance for the stilted and irrelevant curriculum of the day.

Of curious interest is the fact that between 1812 and 1816, twenty-one medical degrees were awarded to graduates of a medical school operated in New York by a Dr. Nicholas Romayne, and in 1827 twenty-seven medical degrees were also bestowed on a New York group led by Dr. Daniel Liasack, this time through the phantom Rutgers Medical College.

In 1816 the college was closed again, but not the seminary, which was the recipient of generous gifts. In 1825 the name was changed to Rutgers College in honor of Colonel Henry Rutgers, an esteemed philanthropist and an elder in the Dutch Church. He had deposited a $5,000 bond with the Church, but the interest was to go to the college, which was reactivated that year with thirty students in attendance. Tuition was now forty dollars a year.

At this time admission required a knowledge of Latin, Greek, and arithmetic. Most students entered with sophomore standing. In other words, the freshman year was a sort of preparatory year for those who did not have the proper standards. Chemistry and natural history entered feebly into the curriculum in 1830. More attention was paid to the library which was open one hour a week and now listed over 2,000 volumes. But the real libraries were in the two new literary societies, Peithessophian and Philoclean, which formed a sort of symbiosis with the staid college curriculum. Most of the students were from New York and New Jersey and were members of the Dutch Church. But money was still hard to come by, and there were still no dormitories.

In July 1840 the Trustees elected Dr. Jacob Janeway president. He refused and in August, A. Bruyn Hasbrouck was chosen. the first layman to fill this post and this was a pivotal period when a decision was made to edge away from Church control. Soon thereafter the full-time faculty was increased to three and the part-time faculty to five. Modern languages were introduced into the curriculum.

The first fraternity, Delta Phi, made its appearance in 1845, and although it aroused a bitter dispute because of the assumed threat to literary societies, other secret societies followed through the years. The money problem continued to plague the institution and, to make matters worse, the enrollment sagged to sixty-five in 1850. But somehow the institution held together, and even managed to increase its services to the students. About a third of the graduates entered the ministry, another third entered law, others became physicians, business men, or teachers.

The Civil War was to usher in an important transformation in the college. The great change came under the presidency of Dr. William H. Campbell, 1862-82. Even during the war a new vitality was felt. New buildings were erected, and the assets of the college increased fivefold in the decade. During Dr. Campbell's presidency, $430,000 came to the college in the form of gifts and bequests.

The Rutgers Scientific School was established in 1864. With the passing of the Morrill Act, Rutgers was declared the land-grant college for New Jersey, having successfully competed against Princeton and the Normal School at Trenton. The college almost ceased being a church-related institution and acquired the coloration of a state institution, even though the formalization of this process was not to take place until almost ninety years later. Two new courses of study were established in the Scientific School: one in civil engineering and mechanics, the other in chemistry and agriculture. Not many students elected these curricula, and very few chose agriculture. However, the new change did mean a bifurcation vis-à-vis the classical curriculum. At this point a single scientific course developed, at first three years in length, later, four. The agricultural curriculum centered on the experimental station and much later in extension courses. Postgraduate courses were recommended by the faculty, and although the number of students involved was small indeed, it is this era that represented the first steps toward an eventual university.

In 1881 another pivotal event took place that was a reflection of the secondary-school movement in the United States: thirteen private academies were approved from which graduates would be accepted by Rutgers.

Sports began to come into the picture, at first a crew, then baseball, and finally football. The famous Rutgers-Princeton game of 1869 was to be the first intercollegiate football game in America. Rutgers won by a score of 6-4, and the red turbans worn by the players marked the first use of color as identification on the athletic field. The era of the literary societies was passing; hereafter the campus heroes were to be the athletic leaders.

Rutgers had come into its own and had become a real asset to New Jersey. There were still financial problems and the college could not draw all the students it needed, but this was a common problem among colleges in the United States for two reasons: first, there were too many colleges, and second, going to college was not a popular choice and would not be until the twentieth century.

With the designation of land-grant college along with the incessant need for funds, Rutgers was to acquire a dual character before the end of the century. The college faced problems up to 1956, when a sharply defined decision was made to make it a state university in fact as well as in name. For more than a period of seventy or eighty years, Rutgers tried to retain its character as a classical college and at the same time to carry out its duties as a land-grant college serving the state. The successor to Dr. Campbell, Dr. Merrill Edwards Gates, was inclined heavily toward the first role. He stiffened standards in admission and in academic performance. He brought in new professors, not one of whom was a clergyman, and practically all had doctorates. The library was strengthened. Compulsory physical training was introduced. Delta Phi erected the first fraternity house in 1887, representing a great change in the living habits of the students. Most important was the building of a dormitory in 1890, the first in Rutgers history.

But the deficits were still there. Dr. Gates tried to get funds both from federal and state sources. The land-grant designation was costing the college more than it was receiving through the state. To make matters worse, the farmers were complaining that the so-called agricultural college, a part of the Scientific School, was not attracting students. Hardly visible was the splendid instruction and research of outstanding biological experts added to the college staff through funds from the Hatch Act of 1887 and the second Morrill Act of 1890.

It is true that the state gave money for a New Jersey Hall, but it was technically under the jurisdiction of the State Experiment Station. To its credit the building had chemistry and biology laboratories for the students. Thus began a jumbled hybrid situation whereby Rutgers was and was not a state institution. Another complication was that the college had established forty free scholarships in 1864 for the Scientific School. In 1888 thirteen more were created. This meant that about three-quarters of the students in the Scientific School paid no tuition. In 1890 the state passed a bill whereby Rutgers was to receive $174 for every scholarship awarded in the State Agricultural College, which was a component of the Scientific School. The only trouble was that this money was to come from the state school fund after all other appropriations had been met. There never to be any such surplus available. Rutgers admitted thirty-three such scholarship students, but when the bill was presented, the state comptroller refused to pay it. In the meantime, a significant change was taking place in the character of the students. The proportion of Scientific School students had increased so much that it was twice that of the classical studies. Electrical engineering was added to civil and mechanical engineering, and a biology major was introduced. Unfortunately, rarely did a student sign up for agriculture. In 1890 Dr. Gates resigned to accept the presidency of Amherst. Curiously, while he had been primarily interested in the Classical College, he achieved his greatest results in strengthening the Scientific School.

The new president, Dr. Austin Scott, tried to resolve the difficulties with the state, but the fact remained that the state was loath to provide money for a private, church-related institution. This added to the gripe of the farmer and created an intolerable situation for Rutgers. While at Princeton the number of students was increasing steadily, at Rutgers it was another story. In the 1896 graduating class there were only fifteen classical and forty scientific students. Desperate measures were devised to attract students. Since the growing educational system in New Jersey needed teachers, a pedagogy course was started. Then a Latin-scientific curriculum was instituted. Entering students were excused from Greek but had to offer two years of modern languages and two years of physics and chemistry. A new dimension was added to the college in 1894 by a gift of a gymnasium from Robert F. Ballantine, a trustee. Finally, the state agreed to pay $80,000 of the $131,610 for the scholarships that had been given out. It was really the second great victory in clinching what was later to be the creation of a state university. However, in order to settle the legal aspects, the state and the college agreed to a suit that the college happily won.

Another important precedent was set when the state,

through the State Agricultural College of New Jersey, agreed to provide $12,000 for a ceramics laboratory and $2,500 for animal operating expenses. In 1904 Mrs. Ralph Voorhees donated a new library to the college, which now remained open eleven hours a day. The next year Dr. Scott retired as president, having survived one of the most trying periods in the history of the college.

By the early part of the twentieth century, Rutgers was still a very small college. Princeton had five times as many students and other Ivy League colleges numbered many more. In 1906 Dr. William H. S. Demarest was the first alumnus of Rutgers to become president. It was he who really brought about the State University of New Jersey concept.

In 1906 the state allocated money for the establishment of short courses in agriculture and related industries at the Experiment Station. A new building was constructed at the College Farm and new professors were added. It had taken a long time for a pattern to develop, not exactly that envisaged at the time of the original Morrill Act, but in essence much more useful to the agrarian part of the population and to the general welfare of the state. In 1914 the state appropriated $100,000 for a large administration building, and in 1918, through the Smith-Hughes Act, the training of teachers of agriculture for high schools was added.

On the high school level New Jersey had been forging ahead perceptibly, and the time had almost come when every boy and girl could be sure of a high school education at public expense. The only normal school in the state prepared teachers for the elementary school. It was Rutgers that now moved into the preparation of teachers for the secondary-school system, thus supplying a second great service to the state.

Toward the end of the first decade new buildings were

added in engineering and chemistry, and this, too, was another service to the state, serving the burgeoning demands of doctoral programs, which were also added in chemistry and biology. Research and scholarly publications moved apace.

President Demarest spared no efforts toward cementing the relationship with high schools throughout the state, and as a result four-fifths of the entering students were from public high schools, whereas thirty years before, the proportion was one-fifth from these high schools. Many of the students were on state scholarships, and this, too, emphasized the public character of the institution. Year by year the state increased its commitment to the college. Each year there was a forward step, as, for instance, when an appropriation was made in 1911 for equipment for the entomology and physics courses.

By 1917 only one-third of the income came from tuition and two-thirds equally from federal and state sources. That same year the State Agricultural College, which was really the Scientific School, was designated as the State University of New Jersey. It was a confusing situation inasmuch as the university was now a part of the college. The specter of the church relationship still hovered over the scene, since the president still had to be a member of the Reformed Church and there still had to be a professor of divinity. In 1920 the trustees decided that there should be a complete break with the Church in order to preserve the character of a public institution. This year, then, was another pivotal year in the history of the college.

During the second decade new buildings were added and more land was acquired through benefactions, but the college still operated at a deficit and its debt increased. Valiant efforts to raise money and secure foundation grants had little success.

In 1918, as a result of vigorous efforts of the State

Federation of Women's Clubs, there was established the New Jersey College for Women as a department of the State University of New Jersey, with Mrs. Mabel S. Douglass, its principal promoter, as dean. This move added still another dimension to Rutgers's role as a public institution for the state, in recognition of the need for women's education.

The College of Agriculture emerged as a separate entity in 1921. Actually, it had been a department of the State University of New Jersey, and the "University" was really an Agriculture and Mechanics or land-grant unit set up under the original Morrill Act. It made sense to separate it as such, inasmuch as it was the direct recipient of federal and state funds. Strangely, while the research and experimental work multiplied, the number of students dropped.

The title *university* for all the elements of the institution was not adopted until 1924. Now what had started as a classical college evolved as the College of Arts and Sciences, and as part of the University there was a College of Engineering, a College of Agriculture, a School of Education, and the New Jersey College for Women.

In 1920 the last vestige of denominational reference was removed, and this strengthened Rutgers's claim as a state university, although legally it was still a private institution. The university's position was still shaky because whatever funds were granted to Rutgers through the State Board of Education meant that much less for the public schools, causing resentment at the intrusion into their share.

In spite of certain frustrations things were moving forward: contributions, foundation grants, the strengthening of the liberal arts program, more students, better facilities. But the whole problem of the dual nature still remained. On the one hand, Rutgers felt that the state should support its services adequately; on the other hand, it did not wish to lose the autonomy and freedom of a private institution.

In 1924 Dr. Demarest resigned, fatigued with the unsolvable problems that lay before him and also realizing, perhaps, that the days of Rutgers as a private institution were numbered. But just as Dr. McCosh had fashioned Princeton into a university, so Dr. Demarest had developed Rutgers into a university.

Dr. John Martin Thomas, the next president, accepted fully the responsibility of the institution as a land-grant college and as the State University of New Jersey. As an aside he also mentioned the retaining of the "traditions of the historic Rutgers." There was the same old difficulty that was to linger on for another generation. Hereafter, an executive committee working closely with the president was to be an innovative change. For the first time the state appropriation rose above $1,000,000, but the important aspect was that funds for the College of Arts and Sciences were now included. No longer was the state limiting itself to the land-grant part of the university. Energetically, President Thomas kept hammering away in public speeches on the services of Rutgers to the state. A campus plan that was to be a forerunner of the eventual greater university was started. Most important was the survey made by the United States Bureau of Education to map out the needs of the state and the role of Rutgers in meeting those needs. But the trouble still lay in the fact that the annual appropriation for Rutgers still came from the same main-stem tax that served all the other state educational agencies. The more Rutgers received, the less they received. All complained that Rutgers was not a state agency and that it was run by a private board of trustees. To meet the latter criticism the board voted to include, ex officio, the chancellor, the president of the Senate, the commissioner of education and the president of the State Board of Education. A campaign to institute a state mill-tax for Rutgers failed. President Thomas was ready to give the state a majority on the board of trustees. This the board of trustees was unwilling to do and felt, moreover, that it was illegal to abandon this power to the state. At the same time some voices within the state argued for a completely new state university.

At this juncture the state appointed the so-called Duffield Commission to examine the whole problem de novo. As a result, a state board of regents was created to deal with the needs of the state and ways in which Rutgers could supply these needs. State scholarships were ended, and the money was to be used to reduce tuition fees for all New Jersey students. The title of *State University* was repealed. The same problem was still plaguing both the university and the state: how to preserve the private character of Rutgers and still serve the state. Fortunately, in spite of these serious arguments, the university was inexorably moving ahead, in enrollment and in services, especially in the School of Education, since the normal schools did not become four-year institutions until 1935. The School of Education was rendering tremendous service to the state and enrolling thousands of students, not only in its summer session but in forty-two extension centers throughout the state, and also through its masters and doctoral programs. In 1927 an existing College of Pharmacy in Newark was incorporated into the University. It was the first step in what was to be the Newark complex, at a much later date.

In 1929 the College of Arts and Sciences re-formed its courses so that the first two years made up a general course while the senior college was devoted to a major and a minor. This represented a great change from the original pattern of a classical curriculum with almost biblical overtones, and while it was still a liberal arts course, it was somewhat vocational and preprofessional in orientation.

Amidst these changes there were turbulent moves to organize the University Faculty, but because of the strong pull for autonomy by both the College of Agriculture and the New Jersey College for Women, the cohesive move was frustrated. The character of the student body began to reflect the changing character of New Jersey citizens. Originally almost entirely Protestant, by the thirties about one-fifth was Roman Catholic and another fifth, Jewish. And so, as the depression years were approaching, Rutgers had become a complex, many-faceted university changing deeply from a small private institution to an almost wholly public one. In December of 1931 Dr. Robert Clarkson Clothier became president.

To be or not to be a state university? Dr. Clothier could not see the possibility of a complete break. Rutgers was a private institution with extensive relations with the state. The trustees agreed with this philosophy. But now financial woes hit the state. The railroads withheld forty percent of their contribution to the main-stem taxes that supported education, including Rutgers. The university lost twenty percent and then ten percent more of its state appropriations. Salaries were slashed: positions were dropped. The effect of the cuts was mitigated by a strong and successful campaign by Dr. Clothier to restore the original appropriations, but then student enrollment began to drop. Happily, in 1937, the state reestablished state scholarships, which reached $200,000 in a few years. The Federal Emergency Relief Administration helped the situation at Rutgers, as at most colleges, by providing part-time job opportunities. Then the National Youth Administration continued this all-important student help program. It was a gloomy period for most colleges, as it was for the nation, and yet the mettle of the institution was tested and it was not found wanting. Adjustments were made and the faculty's economic position was severely affected. Tenure had not been established and there was no solid pension system. Despite these shortcomings, the faculty held strong. The Graduate Faculty was created in 1932, and this was a major organizational change because this faculty exercised control over masters and doctoral courses. This in turn encouraged productive scholarship and research. Two aspects of this evolution were the establishment of the Rutgers University Press and the University Research Fund. There was a greater selectivity of students, and by 1940 Rutgers was in the top five percentile in this respect.

In 1934 a University College was established to give part-time evening courses both in Newark and in New Brunswick. The following year the Graduate School of Banking was established with home-study courses throughout the year and an intensive two-week summer session. This was a three-year course and drew participants from the entire country.

Through the Works Progress Administration an addition to the College of Engineering was completed and other campus beautification projects and internal improvements were effected. But, because the trustees were loath to increase the indebtedness of the university, an opportunity to receive $2,000,000 for new buildings through the Public Works Administration, almost half of which would have been a grant, was missed. As the depression decade neared its end, Dr. Clothier, who had aspired to a liberated Rutgers with an endowment of about $30,000,000 so that it could exist free of any dependence on the state, was forced to admit because of fund-raising failure that the only way Rutgers could survive would be to strengthen its partnership with the state. Happily, the relationship with the state was working out amicably, especially since the Board of Regents set up by the state to oversee its appropriations had softened its attitude on providing an overall umbrella for all higher education within the state. The Regents even suggested that the state should provide capital funds for Rutgers.

But soon the university was caught up in the throes of reorganization for the War. Civilian enrollment plummeted, but Rutgers became one of the pilot schools for the Army Specialized Training Program. The campus became geared almost totally to the war effort with a number of government-sponsored programs in action. It was a valiant period in other respects, too, for over 6,000 Rutgers men and women served their country; 234 gave their lives, including Dr. Clothier's son.

But the war was to offer an opportunity for a break with the past. Under a plan adopted on March 26, 1945, Rutgers was to be known as the State University of New Jersey and four state officials plus five public members were to be added to the board of trustees. An annual appropriation was to be made, and employees of the university were to be included in the State Employees' Retirement System. The Board of Regents was abolished.

During the following year a new dimension was added by happenings in Newark. There had been a group of colleges in Newark known as the Dana group, which included the New Jersey Law School, founded by Richard D. Currier in 1908, a pre-law division known as Dana College, and the Seth-Boyden School of Business, all proprietary and all in one building at 40 Rector Street and owned by Currier. In 1936 they had merged with the Newark Institute of Arts and Sciences and the Mercer Beasley Law School to form the University of Newark. The university encountered financial difficulties during and after the war. On July 1, 1946, it merged with Rutgers and became known as the Newark College of Rutgers, including a College of Arts and Sciences, a School of Business Administration, a Law School, and a College of Pharmacy. It was a step closer to the concept of a public university. An almost explosive rise in enrollments occurred after the war with the equated full-time enrollment at 16,000 by 1948. A temporary campus was organized at Camp Kilmer. In 1969 this became an innovative and experimental college and among its goals was an attempt to aid disadvantaged groups. Off-campus centers were created in Morristown, Englewood, West New York, Trenton, and Atlantic City, and the University College established a new division at Paterson. In 1950 Rutgers absorbed the College of South Jersey, which had been founded in 1926 by Arthur E. Armitage as the South Jersey Law School, and this became the nucleus for a permanent new Camden campus.

The needs of Rutgers, especially for new buildings, were rising steeply. Unfortunately, a $50,000,000 bond issue for Rutgers and other state colleges and agencies was defeated by the voters, mainly on the private school issue. Declining enrollments added to the many problems facing the institution. In 1951 Dr. Clothier decided to retire, having served longer than any of his predecessors and having led the university through the most chaotic period brought about by changing conditions affecting all universities, not Rutgers alone.

He was succeeded by Dr. Lewis Webster Jones. His stance was not on partnership with the state but on fulfilling its role as a State University. A $4,000,000 appropriation was made by the state for a new library, and $2,000,000 was appropriated for agricultural facilities; also $1,000,000 for a library at Camden. But so much more was needed that it was decided to borrow $3,500,000 and later to negotiate for loans for dormitories through the Housing and Home Finance Agency. Educational developments were proceeding apace, however, and a Graduate School of Social Work, a Graduate School of Library Service, a Graduate School of Education, and the Eagleton Institute of Politics were established during the decade of the fifties.

On June 1, 1956, there was duly passed by the Legislature, with the consent of the Rutgers Board of Trustees, and formally sanctioned by the New Jersey Superior Court, an act that established a publicly controlled Board of Governors. This was a fundamental change for Rutgers, for six of this new board would be appointed by the governor and five by the trustees from among their members plus the president of the university and the commissioner of education, ex officio. The board of trustees remained in an advisory capacity and also as fiduciary agents of the university assets of some $50,000,000 that, however, were at the disposal of the governors. The control had now been transferred to the state, and Rutgers was now dependent on the state for its existence, but with an academic autonomy that boded well for the future. Two loose ends were amicably settled: the scholarship funds for students for the Dutch Reformed Church ministry were turned over to the General Synod of the Church, and the Rutgers Preparatory School was severed from the university. On August 15, 1958, Dr. Jones abruptly submitted his resignation. It had been a hard battle, and in spite of physical growth and educational developments, the adjustments with the new board of governors, with the state, and with his own administrative staff had taken its toll. Dr. Mason W. Gross was elected president on February 27, 1959. A new era was ahead for Rutgers through a bond issue happily passed in 1959. This, plus another $17,000,000 through federal help and gifts, made it possible for Rutgers to be physically transformed as it had never been before, with a new general classroom building, another one for education, a dormitory complex, a gymnasium addition together with new facilities for biology, physics, and engineering. The Newark campus really moved forward with a Law Center, classrooms, and laboratory and library facilities of its own. Both Camden and Douglass College (the new name for the College for Women) received needed buildings. Full-time enrollment doubled to almost 12,000; part-time almost doubled to 7,000. A second bond issue for higher education gave Rutgers another $19,000,000. In 1961 a two-year Medical School was a major advance. By 1965 research sponsored mostly by the government rose to $12,000,000. There was a bewildering but healthy change in higher education in the nation, in New Jersey, and particularly at Rutgers, the State University.

One might say that Rutgers has gone through four stages. It started as a small, church-related school for men. Then, after the Civil War, it began to evolve as an institution serving the state, even as it was losing its church coloration. Next, it began to spread modestly in Newark and established itself as a somewhat different type of multicampus institution while managing to retain its small basic men's college. Finally, after World War II, as a full statewide university, it numbered five major campuses, a panoply of doctoral programs and research activities, fulfilling in every way its major role as a great state university. In fifty years, current fund expenditures have increased from about $2,000,000 to $178,559,811.

Its New Brunswick campus is really composed of two major campuses with a number of radial areas, such as the College of Engineering, one of the great engineering colleges of the country; the College of Pharmacy, also second to none; Douglass College, which has been mentioned; and Livingston College, a prime example of an integrated institution.

Its Camden campus has evolved into a major operation. The Newark College of Arts and Sciences is a complete university in itself. It includes among other units, the College of Nursing. The Cook College campus of the University would make the originators of the land-grant college burst with pride in seeing how an outstanding agricultural research center has blossomed from humble beginnings. Its University College, which includes the evening session and part-time arrangements for thousands of students, has an enviable record of not denying any legitimate request for service.

The ten colleges make up the complex known as Rutgers, the State University. It took a long time, two wars, and a depression to straighten out the complicated organization, and some heart-rending decisions took place along the way. But now it's there—a state university that is the pride of New Jersey.

4
Theological Colleges

IT HAS BEEN shown how each of the two colonial colleges was really a symbiosis of a theological college and a college of liberal arts. This pattern took place in the case of every private college until the formation of Rider College in 1921. Before that, a college was either a public college or a church-related one. I shall take up the two theological seminaries that came out of the two colonial colleges and then proceed to a brief discussion of those theological colleges existing at the time of the writing of this book.

All of these seminaries and theological colleges prepare spiritual leaders for their respective congregations, whether Protestant, Catholic, or Jewish. While at the beginning the Protestant colleges were heavily committed to one particular sect, as time went on and the number of students dwindled, the doors were opened to those of other Protestant groups. Even in the Catholic grouping, they tended at first to be mainly for one particular order, but this particular aspect also disappeared. The diocesan Immaculate Conception Seminary, however, at least in the beginning, was involved with the training of diocesan priests alone, and not open to other orders.

Princeton Seminary

The College of New Jersey (now Princeton) and the Princeton Theological Seminary, as seen above, really grew in symbiosis at the time of the founding of the former. What was not mentioned is that the religious institution grew out of the famous Log College, which had been established by William Tennent in Neshaminy, Pennsylvania, as early as 1726. In 1746 this college, whose purpose was to train ministers for the Scotch and Irish immigrants of the Presbyterian faith, became a part of the College of New Jersey. But the Church felt that the college was becoming too secular, and the college felt that the dictates of religious training were a restrictive influence.

In 1811 the General Assembly therefore decided to establish the Princeton Theological Seminary as a totally separate institution. At first, the seminary students, all three of them, were taken care of in Nassau Hall. Dr. Archibald Alexander was the sole faculty member when these first students began their work.

The Presbyterian Church, having decided to erect its own buildings, the students moved into what is now known as Alexander Hall in 1817.

Slowly but surely the theological school grew into a force that was to dominate Presbyterianism in the United States for more than a century.

The seminary was never intended to be a large institution, but over the years gifts made it possible to add to the "old Seminary" building. A chapel was added in 1834. The original, small Lenox Library of 1843 and its 1879 addition was replaced in 1957 by a more spacious Library with 400,000 books. Stuart Hall, a much-needed classroom building, was established in 1876. Hodge Hall, another dormitory, was completed in 1893. The Whitely Gynmasium was added in 1929. There were a number of other buildings, but Tennent Hall is the one that deserves special mention because it enshrines the memory of William Tennent who founded Log College, the lineal ancestor of both Princeton University and Princeton Theological Seminary. Incidentally, in 1944 Tennent College of Christian Education of Philadelphia formally turned over its assets in trust to Princeton Theological Seminary.

The programs of study include a Master of Divinity sequence in which biblical studies, history, and theology are the main components. There is a cooperative program leading to this degree from Princeton Seminary and a Master of Social Work from Rutgers University for those who wish to integrate the two fields. A separate degree of Master of Arts is available for those striving for professions in Christian education.

A Master of Theology course has been organized for those who wish to extend their preparation for the ministry beyond the Master of Divinity degree. Curiously, special arrangements have been made with the Roman Catholic Diocese of Trenton to train personnel needed by the Catholic Church.

Two doctoral degree programs are also given, a Doctor of Ministry for those actually engaged in full-time ministerial practice, and a Doctor of Philosophy, given mainly to those on independent scholarships or those who plan to teach in higher education. Work is offered in five areas: biblical studies, history of Christianity, theology, religion and society, and practical theology.

New Brunswick Theological Seminary

One would also have to think of Queen's College as a symbiosis, for while one group was interested in the role of the college open to lay students, the Dutch Reformed

Church was thinking mainly in terms of the training of ministers for its needs in America. Let me take up that part of the story from the church point of view, for it is this aspect that led to the separate institution known as the New Brunswick Theological Seminary.

The process repeated itself in other Protestant colleges and, in a somewhat different fashion, in some Catholic institutions. As the Dutch spread in the New York-Long Island-New Jersey area, they naturally wanted their own Dutch Reformed churches. There came a time when there were not enough ministers from abroad, and here and there congregations asked that certain persons be ordained as ministers by the central ordaining body (or classis) in Amsterdam. Sending people abroad for training was time-consuming and expensive. An American Coetus (pronounced *See-tus*) was formed in 1737. There now developed a schism within the Church between those Dutchmen who felt that ministers could be trained in the new country and those known as the Conferentie who felt strongly that ministers should be trained in the mother country and according to strict orthodox principles. Please remember in passing that services were completely in the Dutch language.

At any rate, it is known that a first charter was granted in 1766 to the small group that wanted to establish a college that had a double purpose: to train ministers for the Dutch Reformed Church and to provide a classical education for young men. It must be remembered, however, that as far as the Church was concerned, the first aim was much the more important. And, when one says *Church* one must distinguish between the hierarchical body in the home country that looked upon the new American institution with disdain as opposed to the body of churchmen in America who felt a growing sense of independence. As part of this feeling, the Coetus was beginning to ordain ministers freely.

In passing, it is curious to note that John Witherspoon,

newly elected president of the College of New Jersey (later Princeton), paid a visit to Utrecht and evidently proposed the establishment of a Dutch theological chair at Princeton.

Finally, in 1771, an uneasy peace was established by a meeting in New York. At a general assembly of the Church at Kingston, New York, it was agreed to "settle" a professor at the new college in New Brunswick. But all along there were those who felt that the new college should be entirely a seminary. They even wanted the institution to move to Bergen, nearer to most of the churches.

At any rate, the symbiosis continued. Those who were training for the ministry took their own courses in the seminary section of this wobbly new institution.

In 1816, when the college ceased to function, the General Synod of the Church carried on the theological education. This Synod also held title to the college building that housed the college, the grammar school, and the theological institution. The theology professor usually taught in the college as well as the seminary, since hands were desperately needed.

The physical separation of the Seminary from the College was made possible by a gift from Mrs. Anna Hertzog. A theological hall on a new site was dedicated in 1856. It contained lecture rooms, library, chapel, living quarters and a dining room. This, then, was really the beginning of a new institution. It had been loosely plastered to the College, now it was physically on its own. From this time on it was easier for the seminary than for the college to get gifts for its own endowment and new buildings. Perhaps people felt that gifts for religious purposes insured a more favorable treatment for the hereafter. At any rate, while the college languished in 1873, a $100,000 gymnasium and classroom building for the seminary was made possible mainly through the generosity of Mr. James Suydam of New York. Another generous contribution was made by

Gardner A. Sage and a library in his name was dedicated in 1875. An excellent endowment was in the making, and the years 1856-84 were known as the golden years of the Seminary. But the comfortable independence of the seminary unfortunately drew it away from the churches themselves.

Then a new Dutch immigrational wave directed itself to Michigan, Illinois, Wisconsin and Iowa. Just as the original groups in the East felt that it was too far to have ministers trained in the Netherlands, the churches toward the West felt that they ought to have their own seminary. In 1884 the Western Theological Seminary was founded. Now there were two seminaries to train ministers for a relatively small group of congregations.

An Americanization process was taking place—the word "Dutch" was dropped from the corporate title of the church in 1867. Gradually, English was substituted for Dutch in the church service.

In 1884 five chairs had been endowed, as well as the major buildings. The seminary was in a strong financial position, much stronger than that of Rutgers, from which it had parted. But by the turn of the century it was forced to go back to the churches to seek contributions. The old and aristocratic Dutch families were passing away or losing their desire to bequeath magnificent gifts. This need for money had a good effect. It reminded the seminary that its major purpose was to serve the churches, and it made the churches aware of the role of the seminary, encouraging them to remember it in their budgets. By 1952 contributions had reached $47,315 a year.

It is well to remember that the course of study at the seminary had always been regulated by the General Synod of the Reformed Church in America. At the end of three years of study, the candidates were examined, licensed, and ordained by the Church. Field work and practice in preaching, at one time frowned upon, became a method of enriching the curriculum. In 1892 Rutgers voted to confer the degree of Bachelor of Divinity upon those seminary students who took extra courses at the college. This was a great academic step forward. In 1925 Dr. William H. S. Demarest, upon retiring as president of Rutgers College, assumed the presidency of the seminary. He had always been a minister of the Church as well as a professor of theology. The two events pointed out the fact that although the two institutions were separate, a relationship still existed between them. Under the leadership of Dr. Demarest, the seminary forged ahead educationally, spiritually, and administratively.

The seminary, in the last few decades, has had an outstanding record among the major seminaries of the United States and has received a top accreditation rating. It has assumed leadership in the establishment of foreign mission programs in Arab countries, India, Japan, the Philippines, and Hong Kong. Even though it supplies ministers mainly in the eastern section of the United States, many candidates come to it from the West. Most colleges and universities accept the credits earned at the seminary toward degrees at their own institutions.

The history of the seminary is a good example of how seminary classes attached to a Protestant college split off and finally evolve into a full-fledged seminary.

Northeastern Bible College

The Northeastern Bible College is an example of the Protestant Bible colleges that were formed in various parts of the United States. There are about two hundred now in existence, and about half are accredited institutions.

Dr. William L. Pettingill started what was then the Northeastern Bible Institute in 1950 in the Sunday School rooms of the Brookdale Baptist Church in Bloomfield.

There were about a half dozen students. In 1952 the Institute was able to acquire a 17-acre estate in Essex Fells, with dormitory facilities for 150 students.

Northeastern is accredited by both the American Association of Bible Colleges and the Middle States Association of Colleges and Secondary Schools. While it is interdenominational, the majority of the students are Baptist, and the proportion of men and women is about even. This institution is an undergraduate college, although it does offer a fifth year toward the Bachelor of Theology degree. Students study for their bachelor's degree in one of four majors: ministerial, missionary, Christian education, or sacred music. There are about 300 full-time students and about 100 part-time students.

In 1972 the Institute became the Northeastern Bible College. It might be noted that while the college is intended mainly for those who would serve God in the traditional Protestant sphere, there is also the possibility that the curricula of this institution may prepare one equally well for a wide variety of social services. Indeed, there are those who would say that the courses of study prepare one for almost any field, just as they said two hundred years ago. What college curriculum is the true path to wisdom and life service?

Immaculate Conception Seminary

The Immaculate Conception Seminary is located in Mahwah, New Jersey. Like other religious institutions, it had existed since 1861 in symbiosis with a Catholic liberal-arts college, in this case, Seton Hall College in South Orange, New Jersey. In 1926, because of the growing needs of both the college and the seminary, it was thought best to move the seminary to its own campus in Mahwah. The seminary was independently incorporated in 1972 as an educational institution. Two years later it was approved as a Graduate School of Theology. It has two degree courses: Master of Divinity in Pastoral Studies and the Master of Arts in Theology. The former is taken by men who are training for the priesthood, over a hundred of them. The latter may also be taken by men preparing for the priesthood, but it is mainly intended for those who may not be certain of the type of ministry they wish to train for. There may be those who want to specialize in theology for teaching or for some form of spiritual service to mankind. There are about 70 of these students, roughly a third of whom are women. The first group, those preparing for the priesthood, live on campus.

Immaculate Conception is a diocesan institution, and since it is the only Catholic institution of its kind in New Jersey, it is expected that its graduates will serve in the parishes of New Jersey. The bachelor's degree is required for entrance, and most of its students come from Seton Hall. Immaculate Conception also serves different orders of the Catholic Church that may send groups to its campus for special training for the Master of Arts in Theology.

There is a beautiful 735-acre campus and a number of outstanding buildings, including a classroom building, a library, a chapel, a conference hall, and, of course, dormitories for the seminarians.

Saint Michael's

Saint Michael's Monastery is considered a Catholic Theological College, established by the Passionist Fathers as the Saint Michael's Passionist Monastery and duly incorporated by the state of New Jersey in 1866. The prime purpose was to train those who would eventually be serving the Passionist churches.

It is hoped that its graduates will serve primarily in the Passionist Churches of the Eastern seaboard, although some may be assigned to other churches.

At present, there are about twenty-five seminarians in the monastery, which, incidentally, has a sort of affiliation with St. John's University of New York. Entrants must have four years of college and are awarded the Master of Arts degree upon graduation. The course of training covers about four years.

Don Bosco College

Don Bosco College is a good example of a Catholic college for those who are training for the religious life, the counterpart in the twentieth century of Protestant institutions that, one to two hundred years ago, were formed to train ministers for Protestant churches. Don Bosco traces its origins to 1928 when the Very Reverend Richard Pittini, then Salesian Provincial of the Eastern United States, encouraged its establishment in order to train Americans for the Salesian Order. At first the college used the Norton mansion in Newton, but within three years it was necessary to erect a new building. The institution was named Don Bosco Seminary after Saint Don Bosco, who founded the Order in the nineteenth century.

A modern classroom and library building was constructed in 1963. The following year other students besides prospective Salesians were admitted, including Benedictines, Capuchins, and diocesan students. Thus it is an undergraduate college for those who wish to go on to a Catholic school of theology.

An examination of the curriculum shows that the core is theology, philosophy, Latin, English, history, and science, with electives in mathematics, psychology, education, music, and art.

Practically all of New Jersey's colleges have been church-related, and it might be generalized that all of them started for one of two reasons: either to encourage the training of workers for the church, whether as ministers, priests, brothers, or sisters, or to keep the flock together, whether it be Protestant or Catholic.

Alma White College

We have already stated that there have been more church-related colleges in New Jersey than is generally realized, but because they are small and because very little publicity is showered upon them, few people appreciate the fact that the aggregate of all these colleges presents quite a distinct service to the state.

One of these small colleges is Alma White College in Zarephath. Named in honor of Alma White, the founder of the Pillar of Fire, it began to give courses in 1917. There were many small sects in the Protestant Church in the United States, just as there were orders in the Catholic Church. They were interested in the establishment of churches for the preaching of the gospel, in the publication of religious literature, in the founding of schools on all levels to build Christian character among people. Alma White was one of these forceful Protestant leaders. Not only was she an outstanding teacher but also an editor, a writer of hymns, and a social reformer as well.

In 1921 the State Board of Education granted the college the right to offer the degrees of Bachelor of Arts and Bachelor of Science. The college is coeducational and admits students of all faiths and all races. There is heavy emphasis on daily prayer, on Bible study, and on a strict code of moral conduct. In 1974 the college resolved to offer the Bachelor of Theology exclusively. Located on a beautiful rural campus, the college, in spite of its small student body, has a classroom building, a chapel, an auditorium, a gymnasium, and a library.

In the last half-century, there has been a tendency to think of higher education in terms of public institutions, and indeed these account for almost four-fifths of the students in higher education. Nevertheless, the role of church-related colleges in New Jersey is important, and has given higher education in New Jersey alternative opportunities that have not abounded in the West.

The Jewish Colleges

The need to establish schools of theology that arose first with the Protestant churches and then with the Catholic churches did not arise with the Jewish congregations until the middle of the twentieth century, at least as far as New Jersey was concerned.

There are two institutions in New Jersey, both exponents of the Jewish Orthodox stance, and both are dedicated to preparing rabbis. They are Beth Medrash Goveha and the Rabbinical College of America.

Beth Medrash Goveha, located in Lakewood and established in 1948, emerged from the smoldering ruins of the European Jewish community. It was the indomitable spirit of Rabbi Aaron Ketler that led to the establishment of the institution on the nine-acre estate in Lakewood. A three-storied structure that contained the instructional units and a library was added in 1964. A dining hall for 400 students followed in 1965, and a 200-student dormitory in 1969. Beth Medrash Goveha is authorized by the state to award the degrees of Bachelor and Master of Rabbinical and Talmudic Studies. The institution has about 700 students, some single and some married. They come from many different parts of the United States. The curriculum, which includes the Bible, Talmudic studies, codices, ethics, philosophy, history, languages, and finally professional training, may take from five to seven years. Graduate studies are provided for in the Rabbi Aaron Ketler Institute for Advanced Learning.

The Rabbinical College of America was established in 1956 in a modest one family house in Newark as an affiliate of a worldwide Lubavitch movement, which has centers for rabbinical education all over the world, including some ten centers in the United States. Chief Rabbi, Menachem M. Schneersen, of this progressive intellectual movement in the Jewish faith, sent ten students and two teachers to set up a center in New Jersey.

In 1971 the Rabbinical College moved to a new, fifteen-acre campus in Morris Township, New Jersey. It has classroom and lecture halls, a library, dormitories, a dining hall, an auditorium, and facilities for public worship. It was able to expand its program and now has two courses of study, both leading to the degree of Bachelor of Religious Education. The first course of study aims for rabbinical ordination, requires three to four years of Judaic studies, and is four years in length. There are about 160 students in this program. Basic courses include Talmudic studies, Jewish philosophy and ethics, Jewish codes and electives from ancient languages, history, and social science fields.

The second course of study, a New Directions program established in 1972, was created for those who had college or university degrees, who did not have the Talmudic background, but felt a yearning to return to Judaism and to identify with the traditions of their people. There are about 100 part-time students in this second program. In 1973 the college was officially approved by the state.

And so, the cycle is now complete. Church-related colleges, which were established to train for the ministry and, side by side, to train young men for a cultured and meaningful life, became in time different kinds of colleges and lost their religious coloration.

Now there is in New Jersey an important grouping of theological colleges, two of which, Princeton and New Brunswick, have persisted from colonial times; the others, developed in the nineteenth and twentieth centuries, represent the three major faiths and also, one might say, the ethnic makeup of New Jersey. They are not mass-production institutions, but they are all working hard to reach their goals, to provide spiritual leaders—in most cases for New Jersey but also for other parts of the country—who are all outstanding exponents of their religious educations.

5
Drew University

AT PRINCETON and at Rutgers there was the emergence
of nonsectarian institutions after their seminaries separated
into autonomous campuses. At Drew the process was somewhat different. Originally a seminary, the liberal arts component was added later, but this led to difficulties when the
added component became larger than the original seminary.
To begin with, the original institution was made possible
by a gift from Daniel Drew, who, in spite of predatory and
often unsavory tactics in the rough-and-tumble atmosphere
of Wall Street, was a sincere churchman and an altruistic
and generous contributor. In 1866, as the Methodist Episcopal Church was nearing its one hundredth anniversary, there
was a movement to found a seminary for the training of
Methodist ministers. Daniel Drew was prevailed upon to
help, and he gave $250,000 for the erection of a building
and an equal sum for faculty endowment. This was a larger
gift than any other educational institution had received
at that time. The Reverend Dr. John McClintoch, an outstanding leader of the Methodist Church, was selected by
Drew to head the institution. Drew became president of
the board of trustees.

In 1867 the Drew Theological Seminary bought the existing Gibbons estate in Madison for $140,000. It included a magnificent mansion in a beautiful forest setting covering almost 100 acres. On October 16, 1867, eleven students were enrolled. There was no tuition or room rent since faculty salaries and other expenses were paid from the endowment fund, but the food, cooperatively arranged for, amounted to about $150 a year. The course of study was three years in length and led to a Bachelor of Divinity degree. Some of the students were already college graduates, some had no college background, others only a year or two of higher education. On November 6, 1867, the actual dedication took place with all nine bishops of the Methodist Episcopal Church in attendance. In order to attract outstanding scholars, four substantial brick faculty houses were built at a cost of $84,000, a considerable sum in those days. The state charter was not in effect until February 12, 1868. Control was vested in the Methodist Episcopal Church through the supervision of the General Conference. All trustees had to be Methodists and half of them, ministers. The charter contained one extremely important provision: the trustees could "organize faculties of arts, law, literature and medicine" and could change "its corporate name to Drew University." Sixty years later this provision would become very important, and one hundred years later, a crucial financial issue. Apparently, the trustees instructed Drew to invest the $250,000 endowment as he saw fit. Each year, therefore, Drew would send the seminary a check for $17,500, representing 7% interest on $250,000.

Unlike Princeton and Rutgers, all the students were studying for the ministry, and by 1871 there were 104 of them. The faculty was a good one. Within the framework of the endowment income, all expenses were met and even a modest residue remained. But in 1875 Daniel Drew was bankrupt. He paid the $17,500 but declared that he could meet no further payments. The original $250,000 had disappeared. To stave off chaos, the seminary had to embark on a fund drive in order to pay salaries and other expenses. By 1879, $248,421 in cash and pledges had been collected.

The seminary was saved and in good order. Students were coming from many states and even from a number of foreign countries. Faculty members were traveling to Europe and to the Near East. In 1885 a library was built and named in honor of John B. Cornell, the president of the board and a generous contributor. The curriculum was predominantly a religious one, but in 1884 it was expanded to include elective courses in hymnology, metaphysics, English literature, and general history.

In 1888 there were 108 students, 31 with college degrees, but half with no education beyond high school. Classes began on Tuesday morning and continued until 1 P.M. on Friday, in order to give the older students an opportunity to serve weekend churches. This gave them a chance to earn badly needed money and also to acquire experience. The role of philosophic, literary, and religious societies was a congenial part of life on campus.

The graduates of the seminary were forging ahead in the religious and educational world. Twenty-seven members of the first twenty-five classes became presidents of colleges, seminaries, and universities. Five became Methodist bishops, one an Episcopal bishop. Fifty became professors. Many served as missionaries in the far corners of the world.

A combination chapel, administrative, and classroom building was added in 1899. Trustee Samuel W. Bowne gave a gymnasium in 1910, and two years later his will provided for a dining hall reminiscent of Oxford University's Christ Church Hall. By 1911 there were 177 students. In 1913 a Doctor of Theology curriculum was established. A summer school to instruct ministers with little formal theological training was scheduled. In view of the stance of Methodist activity all over the world, a College of Missions was launched, and this was one of the greatest services to the Methodist Church. This program, incidentally included women for the first time.

In 1928 Leonard D. and Arthur J. Baldwin proposed to donate $500,000 for the erection of a building to house a college of liberal arts, with another $1,000,000 for endowment. This was a gift that was to change the whole character of the institution. Because of the provisions in the original charter, it was possible to change the name to Drew University and to establish an all-male college. Now the new liberal arts college was rich, but the cash-poor seminary was in dire straits. As a matter of fact, it had to borrow $20,000 to pay current bills. The Baldwin gift sought to broaden the base of the institution and also to provide badly needed higher education facilities in northern New Jersey. This was quite a different goal than that of providing Methodist ministers for the country and indeed for the world. Moreover, the new undergraduate college could be a feeder to the seminary. The new college was to be known as the Brothers College in honor of the two brothers.

In 1931 another windfall for the new university occurred when the will of Ella Wendel, the New York recluse, was probated. The exact amount of the gift to the university is difficult to pin down, but it was in the neighborhood of $17,000,000 with a certain long-term income straggling in. The gift was to Drew University, but in view of the fact that the Wendel family had for a long time been interested in the seminary, was the intent to have the money restricted to that part of the university? There is here the intensification of the rivalry between the seminary and Brothers College. At that time, 1934, the trustees decided that the legacy belonged to the seminary.

The seminary had been making drastic changes in its curriculum arrangements. It was voted to require a bachelor's degree for admission to the Bachelor of Divinity degree, thus creating a graduate school. Two other degrees would also be given: the Master of Arts and the Doctor of Philosophy.

But the campus was actually divided. The seminary was all graduate, while Brothers College remained undergraduate. The seminary had the money, but Brothers College was developing fast as a first-rate, nonsectarian institution. At Princeton and Rutgers, the seminary had become separate. At Drew, it was too late to effect such a wrenching decision—mechanically, building-wise, and financially. At Princeton and Rutgers, the seminary was less important; Drew was a seminary first, last, and always, with the college of liberal arts tacked on.

In 1937 there was another windfall. Under the Lenox S. Rose will, $600,000 was made available for a new library and $1,500,000 for scholarships. The latter went chiefly to Brothers College.

The War practically depleted the university of students, but the Navy V-12 contract enabled it to pull through. There was a curious twist to this: there were more Catholics on the campus under this program than Methodists, and there were women, too. For the duration of the war, at the request of the faculty, women were accepted at Brothers College, but when the war ended, even though the alumni and students felt strongly that Drew should be for males only, it was voted to make the university coeducational.

In 1948 the college forged ahead of the seminary in prominence and with 150 more students. The $600,000 yearly budget was split evenly, whereas for the five previous years the seminary had been allotted 65% of the funds. It was an uneasy development, and eventually there would be a showdown.

One new and important aspect of the seminary's work

should be pointed out, especially in view of changing socio-logical aspects in the United States. The seminary had been training black clergymen, and by 1952 it had helped to educate 9,000 black ministers in full programs and in sum-mer and extension classes. There had always been a broad point of view with regard to black students, and also for international projects. This was another brave campaign to add to an illustrious record of tolerance and service.

By the mid-fifties the name Brothers College was quietly dropped and the title College of Liberal Arts was substi-tuted. The seminary became the Theological School. New dormitories were built in order to keep up with the bur-geoning needs of the college. In 1958 a $9,000,000 audi-torium-gymnasium-natatorium was completed. That same year, as government loans became available, more dormi-tories, a dining hall, and a university center were made possible. By the end of the decade, eighty percent of the students were in campus dormitories. The original idea of the Baldwin brothers of serving students in northern New Jersey was shifting to a national liberal arts college. Drew was no longer a small college as its enrollment approached 1,000.

A third component was added to the university with a Graduate School including not only elements spun off from theological studies but also elements in literature and his-tory. Unobtrusively, sciences had been coming into the picture as part of the broad liberal arts studies, and, finally, in 1968, a sparkling new science facility was completed. In the framework of the original seminary, this was an im-portant development. The college was growing and achiev-ing national prominence. It was above average in selectivity of its incoming classes. It had the largest proportion of students going on to the doctoral degree in the state. By 1969 the enrollment had risen to 1,242. It had broadened its outside commitments to include a United Nations Seminar, semesters in Brussels and in London, and curricula in marine biology, library science, engineering, and teaching. It was truly an imaginative and ambitious panoply of projects. But the inevitable clash between the theological school and the college had to come, and it occurred under the presidency of Dr. Robert Fisher Oxnam. It was a bitter fight, but out of it all came a new charter for Drew. All references to "Drew Theological Seminary" were struck out, although the theological school was still related to the Methodist Episcopal Church, and at least one fourth of the trustees still had to be Methodists. The two alumni associations (theology and liberal arts) each selected four trustees. Some of these changes were necessitated by government requirements, in that no government moneys could be given to private colleges under religious control. But now the university was one, legally nonsectariarian, with a varied board of trustees. In any case, there was very little money coming in from the Methodist Episcopal Church. All elements had to compete, as they do in any institution, for a proportionate share of general funds. The breach had been healed, and Drew University was a whole, adding luster to the record of higher education in New Jersey, and also serving the nation faithfully and effectively.

6

Two Engineering Colleges

Stevens Institute of Technology

THE Stevens Institute of Technology was made possible
by a legacy left by Edwin Augustus Stevens, in 1867, in
which he left a block of land plus $150,000 for the erection
of a building and $500,000 as an endowment for an
"institution of learning."

The father of Edwin, Colonel John Stevens, had brought
his family to Hoboken in 1794. In 1808, under the direction
of his son Robert, he placed the *Phoenix* in commission, the
first steamboat to engage in ocean travel between Hoboken
and Philadelphia. He also built the first locomotive and
railroad track in America, located on his estate. The two
sons conceived the idea of armor-plated battleships. Edwin,
like his father and brothers, was involved in mechanical
engineering or what was then referred to as "mechanical
arts."

The trustees decided that, in accordance with the interests
of the Stevens family, the new institution should be a school
of technology, and, accordingly, the Stevens Institute of

Technology was created and incorporated in 1870. A beautiful building was erected on the spacious Stevens estate overlooking New York Bay. Professor Henry Morton became the first president, and the basic curriculum decided upon was mechanical engineering. Until then, engineering in other schools was mainly civil and military. The original mechanical curriculum has held, with strong emphasis on basic liberal arts courses, including languages. The physical and chemistry laboratories were undoubtedly the best in the country at that time, and some of the other teaching faculties, as well.

In 1871, when the institute formally opened, there were twenty-nine students in attendance. A series of lectures, the Popular and Technical courses, were also offered in the first year. Here, Stevens led in an early form of both adult and graduate education.

Dr. Alexander C. Humphreys, president from 1907 to 1927, inspired gifts of $4,500,000, and it was he who was responsible for introducing the concept of engineering economics.

In 1930 President Harvey N. Davis established an evening school. He stressed the importance of the humanities and greatly widened the role of research in the institute. Andrew Carnegie, who gave almost $300,000, was among the contributors who aided the school. New departments were added as technology evolved: marine, electrical, chemical.

In 1916 a gymnasium was built and in 1969 an outstanding new library. Other new buildings such as the Morton Memorial Laboratory of Chemistry, the Naval building, the Peirce Laboratory of Metallurgy, and the Kidde Laboratory of Physicals kept the institute in the front ranks of engineering. In the thirties, two dormitories were established, and this, too, stressed the national aspect of the institution.

New Jersey Institute of Technology

The New Jersey Institute of Technology started as Newark Technical School and was authorized by legislative act in 1881 when a group of community and industrial leaders petitioned the city of Newark to provide training for industrial personnel for the growing manufacturing enterprises of the state. The school began as an evening operation in rented quarters in 1885 with Professor Charles A. Colton as director. The students who worked ten hours a day attended classes five nights a week, and the curriculum included science and mathematics. The success of the school led the city and friends to contribute money for a building of its own in 1897. New courses were introduced for specific industries. Finally, a few years before World War I, day courses were added. In 1919 the State Board of Education authorized the school to grant degrees in engineering, and the first such day program began with a class of forty.

While the city's participation has not changed, the state is now the major contributor to the institution. In this case, the same evolution as that of the Newark Normal School has taken place, except that the institute is still an autonomous entity. The state contracts with the Board of Trustees to provide education for a certain number of students each year.

In 1920 Dr. Alan R. Cullimore became director of the Newark Technical School and dean of the college, and it was during this decade that the present overall pattern of engineering education emerged. Five engineering degree programs were included: civil, chemical, electrical, industrial, and mechanical. Evening programs in technical subjects were amplified and, in a way, carried out the original intent of the school founded decades before. During the late twenties, an evening degree program was initiated.

When Dr. Cullimore assumed leadership the school had

only one building. Other buildings were acquired, and with careful nurturing the institution grew in spite of the ravages of the depression decade. The school became known as the Newark College of Engineering in 1930.

The war years took their toll, and immediately following came the chaotic veterans' era, but in the early fifties the decision to stay in Newark was made. It was not an easy decision, for the college was located in a deteriorating neighborhood. But as Newark embarked on its major renewal program in the sixties, Newark College of Engineering was the first campus in the nation to grow through Title I documentation.

The two-acre campus was expanded tenfold and four new buildings were added. Today the campus includes a major classroom and laboratory building, an extensive library, a theater, an immense student center, a gymnasium, and various other sites. Most of this expansion, which established the institution as a major engineering school in the nation, took place under the direction of Dr. Robert W. Van Houten, who was named president in 1949. Among other accomplishments, he developed the graduate program that became one of the largest in the country. Both master and doctoral programs were included.

It is to be noted in passing that this expansion took place almost simultaneously with a similar development of the nearby Newark Center of the State University, the College of Medicine and Dentistry of New Jersey, the Essex County Community College, and the Seton Hall University School of Law. This complex forms one of the most important aggregates of its kind anywhere in the United States and is a good indication of what can be done to stem the deterioration of a large city.

Newark College of Engineering received almost $18,000,000 from the three bond issues of 1959, 1964, and 1968, and about $5,000,000 more from legislative appropriations for new buildings. As the needs of technology changed, the curriculum of the college also developed more sophisticated offerings. The computer-science center, engineering science, and important research projects reflected this development.

In 1970 Dr. William Hazell became president and another great step forward took place. New programs were developed until there were twenty-six scheduled. A new Tiernan Hall was added, opening up new facilities for chemical and electrical engineering. A Bachelor of Technology program was initiated especially for the graduates of the two-year county colleges in both day and evening sessions. A school of architects was started in 1975, the second such school in New Jersey, following the first at Princeton. In 1975 the name of the institution was changed to New Jersey Institute of Technology. That year, the fourth president of the institution took office, Dr. Paul H. Newell.

It can be said that nowhere in the country can one find two institutions, one private, the other public, that have served their state and the nation better than Stevens and the New Jersey Institute of Technology, both alive to the needs of technology, both desirous of training good students, both leaders in the realm of research, both adapting quickly to changing responsibilities, both with above-average placement records.

One must not forget the great contributions of Rutgers in the engineering field, remembering that on the day Rutgers became designated as the land-grant college of the state, it really embarked on what was to be its school of engineering. The development of engineering at Princeton, which started when Dr. Witherspoon bought the first orrery in 1771, was of great national importance, and this, too, helped to make New Jersey outstanding.

To a much smaller and more local extent must be added the Fairleigh Dickinson University College of Engineering. All told, the state has done well in the field of engineering, and one might say that its great industrial growth has been due in no small measure to the dedication of those institutions that have developed engineering curricula.

7

Seton Hall University

MOST of the church-related colleges in the United States were started by Protestant sects. But during the nineteenth century the Catholics began to found colleges. September 1, 1856, saw the birth of Seton Hall College, in a small house in a forty-eight-acre property in Madison, New Jersey. It was named after Mother Seton, who was proclaimed a saint in 1975, the first American-born person to be canonized. The founder was Bishop James Roosevelt Bayley, an Episcopal minister who had converted to Catholicism. It was to be a college and seminary under the direction of the diocese clergy. Tuition was $200 a year. There were five students at the start.

The creation of the college was a difficult endeavor. Bishop Bayley raised a little money in New York, but most of the help came from the Society for Propagation of the Faith in Lyons, France, and from the Leopoldine Society of Vienna. By the July of the opening year forty-four had joined the small college. The first president was the Reverend Bernard J. McQuaid. Madison was too far from the center of Catholic activity, and on April 2, 1860,

Seton Hall moved to a marble villa with extensive acreage in South Orange, paying $35,000 for the building and the property. The college sold its Madison property for $25,000 to the Sisters of Charity, who established St. Elizabeth's College and their Motherhouse there.

By September of that first year the first building was erected. It was a rigorous and disciplined institution. Two sessions of five months each were set up. The day began at 4 A.M. for the faculty and students alike. The course of studies was divided into the classical, English, French, and Mathematics. A student could take not only a four-year course, which was more nearly a preparatory school, but could also enroll in a seven-year sequence, which exists in the present-day college. Almost from the beginning literary societies were encouraged, and they played an important part in the ambience of the school. Ten acres were set aside for sports, and emphasis on physical activities and athletics paralleled the interest in the literary.

On March 8, 1861, the governor of New Jersey signed the legislative act that granted incorporation to the college. It appears there were some laymen on the new board of trustees, but the directive force was still the diocesan clergy. Graduates through the ensuing decades distinguished themselves as princes of the Church and leaders in public life. These were difficult years, but also productive ones, supported by faith and discipline.

The first A.B. degree was granted in 1862, and during that year the enrollment grew to seventy-five. In 1863 a chapel was added, and this also served as a parish church for the South Orange community. In 1866 tragedy struck when a fire destroyed the villa, but by September of 1867 a new three-story building was ready for occupancy.

In 1868 Father Michael Corrigan became president. There were 119 students dispersed among the seven years of the school, plus 17 seminarians and a faculty of 16 only

4 of whom were priests. Students came from different states and from a number of Catholic countries. Oddly, only 16 were from New Jersey.

By 1879 an alumni association had been formed, and its members showed an acute interest in the needs of their alma mater. In 1886 another fire destroyed the college building, which was rebuilt with great financial difficulty. By now, outstanding faculty members were drawn to the institution, both from the United States and Europe. The Reverend William F. Marshall, who was president from 1888 to 1897, seemed to have coped successfully with the problem of reducing the college debt.

In 1897, under the presidency of Father Joseph J. Synnott, the preparatory school was separated from the college, and this, too, represented a move parallel to that of the Protestant colleges. It should be stressed that there had always been and still is a strong relationship between the Bishops of Newark and Seton Hall University.

In 1909 a third devastating fire, this time destroying the classroom and dormitory building, was another setback. But in a year or so a new building had been completed. Now, an important deviation was taking place in the curriculum. Up to 1910 the main emphasis was on classics, history, English, mathematics, philosophy, and religion. After 1910 the growing importance of socialism was reflected in a required course on its nature and history. Soon there was also a greater stress in physical sciences, which eventually led to a science building.

In 1922, under the presidency of Monsignor James F. Nooney, all the land on the north side of the campus was sold in order to meet the debts that had piled up during the disruptive effects of the First World War.

In 1927 an important change occurred. Until then the president of the college had also acted as the rector of the Immaculate Conception Seminary, which was located on the campus. It was during the tenure of the Reverend Thomas H. McLaughlin that the seminary was moved to Darlington, New Jersey. Steps were then taken to ask for accreditation by the Middle States Association, and this was granted in 1932.

During the presidency of Dr. James F. Kelley a great many changes occurred. In 1936 a new dimension was added when courses in accounting, finance, international trade, business law, and statistics were set up. New courses in natural sciences were also scheduled in order to strengthen the premedical and predental curricula. The degrees now obtainable included, in addition to the Bachelor of Arts and Bachelor of Science, a Bachelor of Philosophy and Bachelors of Science in Business Administration, Pre-Medical, Pre-Dental, Physical Education, and Education. This was indeed a change from a few decades before.

In 1937 both undergraduate and graduate curricula were given in the Newark extension in St. Patrick's Cathedral. Another center was opened that year in Jersey City, and, during the same year, the first summer school was conducted at the South Orange campus. Considering that this was a depression decade, all this was an unusual academic tour de force. Another great service was in the nursing field. Seton Hall was not only a leader in New Jersey, but in the whole nation as well. Not the least spurt forward was in the realm of athletics. In 1943 a spacious auditorium-gymnasium was built, and this, too, lent a new aspect to the campus. But even more important was the emphasis on extension education, which was called the Urban Division. In effect, Catholic Seton Hall was a worthy rival of Rutgers, which was trying to decide whether it should really be a state university. At this time women students were accepted, and the first woman member of the faculty, Miss Mary C. Powers, was appointed.

Seton Hall, having survived three previous wars, seems

to have taken World War II in its stride. The veteran period entailed, as in other institutions, a convulsive readjustment. Of the one thousand students at the South Orange campus, ninety-four percent were veterans.

Dr. John L. McNulty became president on March 2, 1949. His was to be another vigorous presidency. In 1950 the college became a university with a College of Arts and Sciences and Schools of Business Administration, Education, and Nursing. The following year, the John Marshall School of Law was absorbed, becoming the Seton Hall University School of Law, with Dr. Miriam Teresa Rooney as dean, the only woman dean of a law school in the United States. Next, the university bought a twelve-story office building in Newark to be occupied by the University College, the new designation for the Urban Division. The following year brought about the creation of the Far Eastern Institute, which acquired a printing press in Hong Kong where Western books and pamphlets were translated and printed in Chinese dialects, and distributed beyond the "bamboo curtain." In quick succession there followed an Italian Institute, an Institute of Irish Culture, a Polish Institute, and an Institute of Judeo-Christian Studies.

In 1953 a two-year community college was established to take care of those students who needed semiprofessional courses. A new building program was initiated that was to change the total look of the South Orange campus, although the 1943 gymnasium had already given it a contemporary architectural aspect. A 500-student dormitory was followed by a $2,500,000 Science and Research Hall, which enabled the university to offer a Master of Science in chemistry. To crown this development, an $8,000,000 library was built.

The Paterson College was opened in 1954 but discontinued later. The nursing program was also developing further and was to become the largest degree program in nursing in the East. Extension courses were given in eleven towns in New Jersey.

The greatest achievement of Monsignor McNulty was the establishment in 1955 of the Seton Hall College of Medicine and Dentistry. It was the first medical school in the state, and it was a brave undertaking spurred on by idealism and the courage of the president. Unfortunately, after ten years of energetic operation, two things happened. The entrenched political situation made it impossible for the university to have control of the clinical facilities of the school. Then, too, the costs escalated far beyond the means of the diocese. Regretfully, the university sold the medical and dental school to the state for $4,000,000, and it became the New Jersey College of Medicine and Dentistry, which, with new infusion of some $189,000,000, built a new medical center and hospital in Newark, opening in 1976.

Finally, in 1976, a new $4,500,000 Law Center was dedicated in Newark for the thousand students in the School of Law. It was the crowning jewel in a long history of devoted service to the people of New Jersey.

8

St. Peter's College

THE SAME basic urge that accounted for the founding of Protestant, church-related colleges played a part in the birth of St. Peter's College. Only in this case it was a Jesuit-inspired move with an admixture of Irish pride that led to a state charter on April 3, 1872. One might say that it was the same sort of church and national pride that had led to the formation of Queen's College (later Rutgers) almost a century before. Because there were few high schools and no parochial schools in the area, a Preparatory Department was organized, but it wasn't until 1878 that a building was finished in Jersey City. This school was closely linked with the St. Peter's parish. The academic year started with seventy-one students in attendance ranging in age from ten to fifteen. In 1889 the first master's degrees were awarded for attending two lectures a week in higher philosophy. A new building was completed near the parish church in 1899.

The college was accredited by the New Jersey Board of Education in 1905, and a clear distinction was made between St. Peter's High School, which had grown out of the Preparatory Department, and St. Peter's College.

The college was closed from 1918 to 1930, primarily because of World War I but also because the Jesuits wanted to concentrate their strength in other institutions such as Georgetown, Boston College, and Fordham. Church-related colleges were not autonomous organisms, and the central order could withdraw a faculty from a college almost at will. The year 1930 was hardly an ideal one to reestablish a college, but start it did, with eighty-five students, in rented business quarters because the high school students completely filled the 1899 building. The academic structure covered religious courses and Catholic prayers, along with a common and basically classical curriculum. Actually, it was the Jesuit Latin and Greek curriculum that was brought to Jersey City.

It was the Reverend Robert Gannon, S. J., who was to breathe contemporary spirit into the institution during the thirties. A fund-raising campaign was launched in 1931, and in 1933 the present campus was purchased for $200,000. The first building, a gymnasium, was completed in 1934, and other buildings followed.

In the day college there was a strong addiction to the single classical curriculum, but the innovation of a business division was started in the evening in 1932. This complex was called Hudson College. Women were tolerated in this evening college, which was the first Catholic college of its kind. The enrollment was growing in spite of the depression, and the evening classes were doing well, although they represented a new departure for the Jesuit fathers, especially since most of the faculty were laymen. Classes started at the present site in 1936, and now that all the classrooms, laboratories, library, and gymnasium were together, one might say that the contemporary St. Peter's was born as of this date.

Like many other colleges, the National Youth Administration, the institutions of R.O.T.C., and the availability of nearby part-time jobs all helped to give substance during the difficult depression years.

Then came World War II, and enrollment plummeted to ninety. Father Dennis Comey, S. J., then president, terminated the master's program in chemistry, which had been an important example of the new type of graduate course. An accelerated undergraduate program was introduced. Hudson College became a wartime casualty. Only the Jesuit, disciplined sense of service and poverty enabled the Reverend Vincent Hart, S. J., to continue the college during the bleak war years. There was one saving factor—much as a lottery had given Princeton a breathing spell over a century before—bingo brought in $2,000 a week. This sum was split three ways—for the church, high school, and college. The faculty toiled around the clock to take care of classes and church duties as well.

The end of the war and the return of the veterans assured the college of success. But it was a changed college, just as other institutions were. The traditional approach to education had evolved into one of more practical import. Hudson College was reopened in 1946, but now it spilled over into the day session. Eventually it was to be known as the School of Business Administration. Accounting, management, and marketing were more popular than religion, philosophy, and Latin, and this chaotic readjustment left its imprint on the revitalized college, even though students still had to take twenty-four credits in philosophy and twelve in theology. A new building arose to take care of the greater enrollment. When the new president, the Reverend James Shanahan, took over in 1949, St. Peter's was a thriving institution.

The assignment of presidents in a Jesuit college is somewhat different than it is in other institutions. During the sixties the Reverend Edward Clark, S. J., the Reverend Leo McLaughlin, S. J., and finally the Reverend Victor

Yanitelli, S. J., succeeded to the presidency. It was under the last named that St. Peter's came nearer to the concept of a college preparing for service in a contemporary world without exactly losing its religious coloration. Many of the students were not Catholic, girls became part of the scene, the turmoil of the outside sociological changes of the community were interpolated into the quiet of the academic setting. In 1972 St. Peter's had 2,500 day students and 2,100 evening students. About $15,000,000 had been spent for a college plant, most of which was less than ten years old. Five laymen were appointed to the board of trustees, and this, too, was a sign of the desecularization of the college.

In 1975 St. Peter's College leased the campus of the former Englewood Cliffs College, which had closed its doors in 1973, and began to develop it as a satellite college for nontraditional students, mainly in liberal arts and in business. A goal of 500-600 students was set. The courses were taught entirely by the Jersey City faculty, who traveled to this new northern campus to give, individually, part-time courses. This also is an example of what is happening in higher education all over the country. Small, private, church-related colleges are finding it difficult to continue, and the religious community is left with a capital development on its hands. Still, a crowded urban institution looks longingly at a peaceful, bucolic setting not too far away with plenty of grass and plenty of parking places.

St. Peter's faces a problem of a different sort than most colleges. It is situated in a city that, like most cities, is eroding in spite of valiant efforts to the contrary. The college itself is located on an extremely small acreage. It has chosen to remain to fight urban blight and to continue as a bastion of service to the local community and to other towns within commuting distance.

9

Bloomfield College

THE ROLE of seminaries in the state of New Jersey has been shown. In the cases of the College of New Jersey and of Queen's College, while there was a relationship to the Presbyterian Church in one instance and to the Dutch Reformed Church in the other, the college unit of the institution was dominant. In the case of Bloomfield, the institution was conceived in 1868 as the German Theological School of Newark, New Jersey. It should be pointed out that there were tremendous waves of German immigrants during the years 1848-60, and this had produced an acute need for Protestant ministers who could conduct services in German for the German-speaking communities. The seminary was affiliated with the Presbyterian Church of Newark, although it was approved by the General Assembly of the Church. It opened in 1869 with three students, six more joining during that academic year. Incorporation by the state of New Jersey did not come until March 13, 1871. Funds were provided by the German churches in the area. Students paid no tuition. Instruction was both in German and in English. At first the school met in the parsonage

hall of the first German Church in Newark, but in 1872 it
acquired the building of the Old Bloomfield Academy,
which had been built in 1810.

The Reverend Charles Eugene Knox was the first president. At this point there were twenty students. More money
began to filter in from churches and individuals, and by
1873, $27,482 was in the school fund. In 1886 a mansard
roof was added, and this provided four new dormitory
rooms, an important step forward.

In 1874 an academic department was established. This
was really a preparatory division to act as a feeder for the
theological school. The term of this department was lengthened to three years in 1875 and to four in 1882 when it
emerged as a partially independent division somewhat
equivalent to a German gymnasium.

With time, as the Germans acquired facility in English,
the need for such special services diminished. But in 1890
a new need arose, that of supplying ministers for Magyar,
Bohemian, and Italian Presbyterian congregations, and
thus the doors were opened to students from other foreign
groups. The change was not without some traumatic effects,
since the moneys contributed had been intended for German
congregations. Eventually, the institution was to serve some
fifteen different language groups. In 1913 it became known
as the Bloomfield Theological Seminary.

In 1914 Knox Hall, a new edifice, arose, built at a cost
of $60,000. It was the first new building since the founding.
The money had been laboriously collected, but the building
was really made possible by a gift of $35,000 from James
N. Jarvie. This was to be the only new building until after
World War I. The difficulties were many, but they were
mainly the same basic problems that all combinations of
college and seminary faced. As a matter of fact, the president at that time, Dr. Harry Edward Richards, expressed
the thought that the college should be discontinued. It was

not closed, and a four-year college course leading to the Bachelor of Arts degree was approved by the State Board of Education in 1923. The idea, as at other seminaries, was to follow the four-year course by a three-year course in theology, leading to the Bachelor of Theology degree. It should be remembered that there was still an academy that preceded the college. In 1931, after the matter had been approved by the Presbytery of Newark and by the General Assembly, the State Legislature approved the change of name to Bloomfield College and Seminary.

With the depression years, the institution underwent the same difficulties faced by other colleges. The situation was not hopeless, for Bloomfield had $648,000 in endowment. The trouble was that there were three institutions to support: the academy, the college and the seminary, all with small enrollments and practically all with students not paying any tuition. When the war came along, the total enrollment dropped to forty-three. Furthermore, the General Assembly of the Presbyterian Church had been reviewing the whole question of seminaries throughout the country. Should they train pastors on a simple, nondegree diploma basis or should there be graduate schools emphasizing the B.D. degree, with the B.A. as the prerequisite? By 1943 the General Assembly felt that the specialized service of the Bloomfield institution was no longer necessary.

The G.I. Bill was to change the complexion of the college. By 1948 the enrollment had increased to 197, with 65 students expressing an interest in the ministry. Courses in business administration were introduced. Regular tuition charges of $400 were instituted, with scholarships for needy students not covered by the G.I. Bill. The academy was discontinued in 1946, but the college was not accredited by the Middle States Association, and soon, as the veteran enrollment petered out in the fifties, new difficulties arose.

In 1955, in a brave decision to continue in spite of

problems, a $500,000 fund-raising campaign was launched. Churches and individuals contributed to its success and two new buildings were made possible, a library and a gymnasium.

Inexorably, a change was taking place. The institution was now more of a college and less a seminary, even though the financial help was still basically church-related. Fortunately, after two refusals, Bloomfield College and Seminary was approved by the Middle States Association in 1961. It was a glorious step forward. That year the registration was up to 556. However, the seminary was not so successful. The term *seminary* was dropped and the term *institute* substituted, and this became a part of the college. In other words, to all intents and purposes, Bloomfield was now a college with the church program as one of the departments. Even this institute work was soon discontinued.

But now that Bloomfield was a college pure and simple, and even though it had dropped all seminary work, it had the same difficulties most private colleges were having. Expenses had shot up enormously, especially faculty salaries. The competition of burgeoning state institutions made it difficult to enroll enough students to meet basic expenses. Furthermore, since the Bloomfield campus was a restricted area, the college had bought a large tract of land, the 338 acres of the Knoll Country Club in Boonton, New Jersey, intending to move there after selling its Bloomfield property. Things got steadily worse, and finally in 1973 the board declared a state of emergency. In 1974, in a move to avoid a crippling deficit, the faculty was reduced by twenty-five percent, and thirteen faculty members were dropped, eleven of whom were tenured. The college almost succeeded in divesting itself of the Knoll property, but unfortunately the buyer canceled the agreement at the last minute, principally because interest had shot up thirteen percent.

The American Association of University Professors instituted court proceedings to prevent the dropping of the thirteen faculty members and succeeded in getting an injunction. The financial situation at this point became intolerable, and a cash crisis forced the college to file for bankruptcy under Chapter XI. A receiver was appointed to apportion income fairly among all creditors. Thirteen members of the faculty had to be terminated, but only seven were tenured and six nontenured. So matters stood in 1975. In 1976 the college succeeded in selling its Boonton property, hoping to solve most of the acute financial problems, providing its enrollment of 600 full-time students plus 800 veterans and 300 evening students held up. But coming out of receivership did not quite solve all the problems, because at that point the tenured faculty that had been terminated had the right to sue. Apparently, the problem has been solved with the help of financial accommodations.

What started as a pure theological school has over the years become a college serving the community, although it does have about 200 boarding students. It is still church minded in a shadowy way because it receives a small amount of money for its community work from the church. It qualifies as a nonsectarian institution legally and in spirit. Under the inspired leadership of Merle F. Allshouse, in spite of the difficulties prevalent, the institution is operating with a new burst of energy and doing effective work in serving the community.

10
State Colleges

GENERALLY SPEAKING, all of the state colleges except the last two, Stockton and Ramapo, were founded pursuant to the New Jersey Laws of 1903, whose purpose was to encourage the establishment of two-year normal schools. One must keep in mind that in the nineteenth century New Jersey was an agricultural state, as a great deal of it still is. It occupies the same position vis-à-vis Manhattan as does Long Island. Indeed, New Jersey was keeping up well with the public education movement, which was best exemplified in New York, Massachusetts, and Connecticut. In fact, in 1828 Professor John MacLean, later president of Princeton, proposed a plan for state aid to education that bears strong resemblance philosophically to what there is today. In 1829 the law appropriated $20,000 for the various counties. In 1837 New Jersey received $746,670 from the surplus in the United States Treasury to be used for education purposes. In 1846 New Jersey had the first state superintendent, and the annual appropriation was increased to $40,000. In 1853 reading clubs for teachers joined and became the New Jersey State Teachers Association. One-week teachers institutes had begun as early as 1849 in Somerville, and they were encouraged and financed by the State.

As public schools developed during the latter part of the nineteenth and the early part of the twentieth century, there developed a need for teachers, and New Jersey decided to establish normal schools.

As early as 1840 one finds evidence that growing communities made an effort to license qualified teachers. This paralleled what was going on in other municipalities, and in 1870 there were twenty-one elementary school organizations.

The eventual development of teacher-training institutions went through four stages: at first as teacher institutes, then as two-year schools, then as three-year normal schools, then as four-year state colleges. The last development was spurred by the veterans' influx after the last war and by the need for more general educational institutions within New Jersey. Before World War II six teacher-training institutions had been founded: Trenton, Montclair, Newark, Glassboro, Paterson, and Jersey City, in that order. While these colleges also supplied teachers for high schools, this function was more or less taken over by the four-year degree courses developed at Rutgers as it evolved as a public institution serving the needs of New Jersey. More secondary-school teachers were also trained at the private colleges, especially after the war.

The first normal school to be established by the state was formed in Trenton, and I shall begin with a history of that school.

The natural interest in education, as urged by national leaders Horace Mann and Henry Barnard, led to the opening of the New Jersey Normal School at Trenton in 1855. This established a pattern for the five other schools that subsequently were formed. Connected with the institution was a model school used as a laboratory for the students. Newark, on its own, established the Newark City Normal School in 1857, and Jersey City similarly established one in 1862.

The second state normal school, established as a result of the 1903 act, was located at Montclair in 1908. The third was to be in Newark in 1913, when the state took control of the existing school. Two things should be noted: first, the demand for trained teachers was so great that the state simply had to do something about it, and second, the population of New Jersey was coalescing in the small, northeastern segment of the state, and it was for this reason that most of the normal schools were to be established in this area. In fact, most of the private colleges were also to sprout in the same area. It should be noted that smaller teacher-training schools were also set up in Bayonne, Hoboken, and Plainfield.

In order to satisfy the southern part of the state, the fourth normal school was established at Glassboro in 1923. That same year the state took over another existing normal school in Paterson and a fifth at Jersey City in 1928. But by 1929 the institution at Montclair became known as the New Jersey State Teachers College at Montclair because it offered a four-year B.A. degree. The institution in the state capital was known as the State Teachers College and State Normal School at Trenton, for it offered a four-year B.S. degree as well as three-year curricula. The other institutions at Glassboro, Jersey City, Newark, and Paterson were known as state normal schools.

But then came the stock market crash and the ensuing Depression. The state normal schools could not expand any more, but in 1935 the names of teacher-training institutions in Newark, Jersey City, Trenton, and Glassboro were changed to State Teachers Colleges since they now offered four-year degree courses. It was not to be until 1951 that a state bond issue was approved to rebuild the six State Teachers Colleges.

In 1953 State Commissioner of Education Dr. Frederick M. Raubinger called together a committee of twenty-four educators representing the six teacher-training institutions and state education officials, to study and reorganize the courses of study at all of the state schools. This committee, under the chairmanship of Assistant Commissioner Dr. Robert W. Morrison, established minimum requirements in general education and also made it possible for students to follow other preprofessional programs in addition to those for an eventual teaching career. This was really the first step in their later development as general colleges. Again, New Jersey was in the vanguard as far as developing a statewide, integrated, forward-looking plan of education. It was the beginning of the evolution of a state college system second to none, and this, together with the almost parallel development of a state university, was to put the state at the forefront in overall state planning of higher education. To be sure, there was bickering among the various segments of education—private, state university, state colleges, and the inevitable tug of small pockets of vested interests. But out of it all came a wonderful forward movement—and in a relatively short period. There was integration and cohesion without interfering with creative impulse and distinctive experimentation.

The greatest problem as the state colleges moved from purely teacher-training institutions to general colleges in the liberal arts mold was that of existing staff. Many of the faculty had been recruited from the public-school system. Now, as the liberal arts were expanded, the source of new faculty had to be different. Naturally, some problems arose between the old guard and the university-oriented appointees. In one case, the struggle became bitter when Dr. Robert Heissler, newly appointed president of Trenton

State College, actually proposed to discharge some of the
old staff in order to appoint the new type of liberal-arts
specialists, but this was before the great expansions took
place. Fortunately, in most cases, the institutions were
expanding so rapidly that there was plenty of room for all.

New Jersey State Teachers College at Trenton

The first teacher-training school in Trenton, New Jersey,
was approved by the legislature on February 9, 1855. In
October of that year fifteen students were on hand for the
opening of the New Jersey Normal School. Tuition and
textbooks were free. In 1846 state supervision was initiated
and compulsory and local taxation for schools was enacted
into law.

Richard L. Field fought for such a school and became
president of the board of trustees. Others on the board
were President John MacLean of Princeton and Judge
Naar, editor of *True American* who helped to keep the
movement out of politics.

The first location was on Clinton Avenue, and Trenton
offered $14,000 to erect a building. The state contributed
$10,000 yearly, increasing the sum to $15,000 in 1872.
The curriculum included English, graphics (penmanship),
bookkeeping, drawing, mathematics, natural science, ethics,
and the theory and practice of teaching. The influence of
Johann Pestalozzi was dominant.

There was a model school attached to the main institution. Women's and men's dormitories were added later.
Gradually, graduates of approved high schools were admitted without examinations. By 1889 the school had 700
students, and by 1890 a new classroom and laboratory
building became necessary. While *normal school* meant the
preparation of elementary-school teachers, the need for

training high-school teachers arose, and it was evident that a four-year course was required. This led to a change in title to Teachers College. In 1925 four-year courses were approved in English, history, science, mathematics, and rural education. Some aspects of the school were provisions for practice teaching, the preparation of music teachers, and, most important, the training of rural teachers, for the state was fundamentally rural. In 1937 all curricula were made four years in length, and the institution was renamed the New Jersey State Teachers College at Trenton.

A new site was secured in Hillwood in 1929, and buildings worth $3,000,000 were erected between 1930 and 1936. By 1940 the campus encompassed 185 acres and 12 buildings. In 1951 Trenton participated in the $15,000,000 bond issue to the extent of $2,041,000.

As more capital became available from bond issues, from the 1963 higher-education law, and from federal dormitory money, more imposing buildings and additions were constructed. By the seventies the institution had about 7,500 full-time students and about 5,000 part-time students. Of all the state colleges it was to have the largest number of dormitory students—about 2,200, which made it, in fact, the largest single residential college in the state. From an institution devoting 99% of its time and facilities to the training of teachers, it now gave over half of itself to other curricula. The inclusion of nursing was responsible for the development of many science courses. The college also seeks to train people for various public-service responsibilities. Four percent of its students come from out of state; only 20% from Mercer County, in which it is located.

Montclair State College

Montclair Normal School was the second such school in

New Jersey and was dedicated in 1908. At the time, the secondary schools in this country served only the intellectually elite. It was not until the thirties that the concept of general education for all affected the high schools. Even at the time of the dedication, probably three-quarters of the teachers in American schools were untrained for their job. Montclair, while preparing elementary-school teachers in a two and one-half-year course, attuned itself to the problem of training secondary-school teachers. Most of the teachers serving in United States schools were graduates of liberal-arts colleges who drifted into teaching. Incidentally, Rutgers was one liberal-arts college that was to tackle the problem of serving the needs of the state in this direction.

The legislature had selected Montclair after considering 64 locations. It had bought 25 acres for $25,000 and appropriated $275,000 for a building to include classrooms, laboratories, library, gymnasium, auditorium, and cafeteria. Dr. Charles S. Chapin became the first principal. There were eight teachers for 187 students, most of them women. By 1913 there were over 500 students. Dr. Chapin soon put his stamp upon the institution and brought in Professor John C. Stone, who had written more books on mathematics than anyone in America, to organize the department of mathematics. Montclair soon became nationally known for its work in this field. Professor Virgil S. Mallory added to Montclair's laurels by keeping up the primacy of the department.

In 1924 Dr. Harry A. Sprague became principal, and within three years Montclair had instituted a four-year course leading to the B.A. degree. Dr. Sprague insisted on a broad liberal-arts background along with the professional courses. It was he who led Montclair into becoming an outstanding college in the country.

By the thirties, a high-chool education for almost everyone was adopted as a policy in this country, and Montclair took the lead in carrying out this policy. In 1937 Montclair was accredited by the Middle States Association of Colleges and Secondary Schools. The school became Montclair State Teachers College in 1958. Under Dr. Sprague the Mental Hygiene Clinic and the Bureau of Field Studies (founded by Dr. Harold S. Sloan) were established. The College High School, a demonstration and teaching laboratory was created in 1929. The college had become nationally known for the discovery of new methods and values. The college participated heavily in the various state bond issues and this has given a new face to what was an old-fashioned architectural style.

The original 25 acres have grown through purchases to 90. There are now 26 buildings including a modern gymnasium, a 1,000-seat auditorium, an additional little theater, and an outstanding library. The fine-arts building is one of the best in the East. The college-union building, with student rooms above it, could well be the envy of any dormitory college in the country. Classroom buildings, science buildings, and dormitories for 600 students are among the 26 buildings on the campus. One of the most pleasant quadrangles to be seen in New Jersey unifies the major buildings.

The third president, Dr. S. DeAlton Partridge, took a leading part in the state fight to have the bond issue passed. He was succeeded by Dr. Thomas H. Richardson who steered the institution through some of the troublesome years. Dr. David W. D. Dickson is now president.

Merged with the college is the Panzer College of Physical Education and Hygiene, which used to be in East Orange and this center contains gymnasiums and a large swimming pool.

Montclair State College has probably had less difficulty in adapting to the concept of a general-purpose college than any of the other teachers colleges for two reasons: first, it specialized in secondary-school majors and this required liberal arts departments; second, because its early principals, notably Dr. Sprague, believed strongly in the value of cultural background. There are now thirty-seven majors to choose from, including fifteen in the humanities and arts, five in the sciences, and others in the social and behavioral sciences. But there are also three majors in business, and this is the inevitable compromise that most colleges make with the priority of liberal arts. Students are interested in jobs and there are simply too many jobs in the business and industrial area for a college to close its eyes to this category of service. Besides, as a multipurpose college, Montclair is training teachers, and high schools need teachers of business as well as those who will teach English or history. One might argue also that business is just as important an approach to the understanding of the contemporary world as is the study of battles and dates.

Montclair is a good example of a college's serving community students and boarding students—an example of a tightly woven, integrated institution, and yet with more outside cultural and international liaisons than most isolated colleges have. It has not lost the disciplinary values of old studies, while it has been adapting to a new, vibrant concept of education. It adds measurably to the service of the state. But it is also a good case study of the ups and downs over the decades of a state-supported institution. When it was built, it was a showpiece. Then followed the Depression years and slow, almost imperceptible physical aging of the buildings, but never of the intellectual processes within the institution. Finally, after a delay due to legislative procrastination, the college received major appropriations that created a "new Montclair." The trouble is that in trying to get a sluggish legislature to move, the public impression given is that New Jersey public higher education is poor, and thus an inaccurate image clings to all institutions within the state. Education at Montclair was never poor; it was always superior. The buildings for a decade or two were not up to par, but this did not affect the educational process. It is time for the general public to realize the excellence of institutions within the state, their cultural sophistication, and their comparatively forward stance. An appreciable number of New Jersey students will still go out of state, but that is due to the fact that the state is small, and if a student is going to go away to college, he inevitably finds himself stepping out of the mythical state line.

Kean College

Kean College of New Jersey really started as the Saturday Morning Normal School in 1855, a teacher-training institution within the Newark School system. It was totally organized, administered, and supported by the Newark Board of Education, which employed its graduates. The board also had to upgrade those teachers already employed in the system, and the board therefore established the Saturday School, where students attended for four years and upon completion of their course received the Principal Grade License, the highest certificate awarded. At this time the emphasis was on basic education since many of the students did not have the benefit of a high-school education. The curriculum included spelling, reading, geography, astronomy, etymology, arithmetic, algebra, geometry, and natural philosophy. By 1877 the curriculum was reduced to two years, and the emphasis shifted to professional courses. In the following year the curriculum was reduced to one year, but in addition the students were required to spend eight weeks on a daily basis in observation and practical teaching. It must be pointed out, however, that simultaneous with these changes admission standards were also being raised and the entering students had in great measure the equivalent of a high-school education. By 1880 high-school graduation was a requirement for admission.

From 1863 to 1876 one sees, quite apart from the normal school, the growth of teachers institutes, and these met jointly with the students of the normal school once a month. One begins to see the influence of Pestalozzi and Horace Mann in the teaching-methods courses, both in the institutes and in the normal school.

As drawing, music, and physical culture made their appearance in the public primary and grammar schools, these subjects found their way into the curriculum of the normal school.

In 1879 the Saturday Morning Normal School became a one-year daily institution, and the name was changed to Newark Normal School. Its aim was still to train teachers for the primary and grammar schools of Newark. A high-school diploma or its equivalent was required for admission. By 1887 the subjects included were mental philosophy, moral science, theory and practice of teaching, general culture, drawing, penmanship, music, physical culture, and lectures on philosophy and science of education, methods of instruction, and training-school practice.

In 1888 the one-year normal school became a two-year course and remained so until 1913, always under the jurisdiction of the Newark Board of Education. In 1901, however, the State Board of Education established regulations for the certification of teachers on a statewide basis, and thus the power shifted from the city to the state. During this period, also, there was a marked emphasis on professional courses. Subject matter was taught in conjunction with methodology. Practice teaching also acquired ever-increasing importance both in the primary school established especially for that purpose and in other schools of the city. The Hebartian influence was introduced through the textbooks by Charles De Garmo and Charles and Frank McMurry.

The principles of Friedrick Froebel and Maria Montessori came in through the courses on kindergarten theory and on primary classes. It could be said that Newark was developing on a par with the best practices in other cities, but, as was happening in other municipalities, the heavy hand of politics also played a role. It should be pointed out that in Newark, as in other New Jersey communities, the professional idealism of forward-looking administrators maintained a modicum of insulated freedom. It should also be mentioned that colleges and universities were giving extension courses for teachers, and this produced a leavening effect on the whole question of teacher preparation and development. Moreover, the school system itself sponsored lectures on teacher improvement. Newark's local Normal School was keeping pace with that of the State Normal School at Trenton. In 1911 the city started to build what was then considered to be an outstanding new building for the Newark Normal and Training School.

In 1913 the operation of the school was taken over by the New Jersey State Board of Education, although the city still owned the building. The name was now the New Jersey State Normal School at Newark. It was a logical move. The expense was becoming too great for the city, and if the state was going to support teacher-training schools elsewhere it made sense to do it for all parts of the state. There was a requirement that graduates had to teach in the public schools of the state for at least two years. Admission standards were raised and some of the courses were upgraded. In 1922 a teacher-training program in manual training was added to the curriculum, and this, too, represented a new trend, especially under the influence of John Dewey. Now, too, since teachers were being trained not simply for Newark but for the state at large, there was a broadening influence, and one begins to observe the growing attention to suburban communities.

In 1929 a third year was added to the curriculum, and in 1934, a fourth year. The name was again changed, this time to New Jersey State Teachers College at Newark, and in 1937 bachelor degrees were awarded for the first time.

But after World War II the building in Newark, beautiful as it was, and a showpiece architecturally in its time, was no longer adequate for its new role as a general college. Hemmed in by a small, deteriorating community, it was hardly possible to fulfill its new role. The institution was bursting at the seams and was awarding the master's degree.

With the bond issue of 1951 it was able to acquire 120 acres in Union. By 1958 the following buildings were erected: classroom, administration, student center, library, and power plant. The transition in offerings and in faculty was more difficult. There were innumerable surveys and discussions, and gradually the format for the new school of arts and sciences began to emerge, reaching a general pattern about 1968. Four general clusters were available to students—humanities, social and behavioral sciences and history, sciences and mathematics, and health disciplines— and students had to take courses in each of the four areas. These areas were also for the purpose of certification on the secondary level. Liberal-arts majors were introduced in 1965. Did the teacher-training courses disappear? Not at all. They were part of the school of education and became intertwined in some cases with liberal-arts majors. It is important to point out that while a student might be majoring in, for example, a science, he could by taking electives in methodology also receive teacher certification in that · discipline. In a world where most students are job oriented, preparing for duty in either a commercial or governmental laboratory and also for teaching had practical advantages. In 1975, out of 1,620 undergraduates receiving diplomas at commencement, 915 had received teacher certification.

In 1956, perhaps in anticipation of the changeover to a liberal-arts college, there was again a change of name to Newark State College, even though the institution was now in Union.

But in the meantime, the erection of new buildings was proceeding apace: a gymnasium in 1956 and a science building in 1958. A small dormitory was built in 1961 and another one in 1963. This represented a new departure, for no longer was the college restricted to commuting students. In 1964 a beautiful auditorium, which also contained facilities for a music faculty, was built. In 1966 another classroom building, a new library to supplant the small one completed in 1954, and a dining facility were added. The fine-arts building was started in 1968. In 1972 an important step forward was marked by an impressive building program that included a new and larger science building, an administration building, a new classroom building, and, most important, four new, large dormitories. The institution could now house one seventh of all its full-time students. By 1975 it had almost 7,000 full-time and 4,500 part-time undergraduate students. It had also 2,500 graduate students in programs that had started after World War II. Forty percent of its students were in the school of education and sixty percent in the college of arts and sciences, but many of these were also being certified for teaching positions. This was a major transposition from the 1,000 students at the time it was a teachers college in Newark.

On October 19, 1973, the name of the institution was changed to Kean College in honor of an old and revered New Jersey family, part of whose estate was in fact the campus of the college. The change of name probably helped to dispel the image of the former teacher-training institution.

Glassboro State College

It was in 1911 that Governor Woodrow Wilson invited Dr. Calvin Kendall to become commissioner of education in New Jersey. Dr. Kendall realized that more normal schools were needed to train teachers for schools in New Jersey, especially for the rural areas. In 1913 the legislature authorized the creation of such a school, in a county south of Mercer. This was the largest area in the East without such a teacher-training school. It took years to see the realization of this move, but finally, in 1917, Glassboro was chosen as the site for the school because it was in the center of South Jersey, because it was a railroad center, and because a nearby high school and elementary school could be used for student teaching. It wasn't until 1923 that the building, after many delays, was finally opened, under the principal-ship of Dr. Jerohn J. Savitz, with an enrollment of 236; all except 10 were women. The school was known as the Normal School at Glassboro. There was even a privately operated dormitory for 22 girls. There were three curricula: kindergarten-primary, elementary, and upper grades. The students had to take basic general courses in English, biology, applied science, geography, history, mathematics, music, speech, and physical education. The basic education courses included psychology, history of education, educational measurements, principles of education, and school management. It was a disciplined two-year school, and strict rules governed the attendance and activities of the students. Tuition and textbooks were free. There were 19 members of the faculty, mostly women.

In 1927 Glassboro was successful in having its first dormitory for 80 girls, and in 1930, a second dormitory for an equal number of girls. In 1928 the two-year curriculum was increased to three.

In 1932, because of the financial stringency caused by the Depression, students were first charged $50 per year, then, a year later, $100. The free use of textbooks was also discontinued. Faculty salaries were reduced from two to nine percent during the period 1932 to 1938. The state appropriation was cut from $173,000 in 1931-32 to $86,000 in 1933-34. Fortunately, many students were helped by the Federal Emergency Relief Administration and later by the National Youth Administration.

Glassboro's importance lay in the fact that it was a leader in the training of teachers for rural schools. One has to realize how wide the expanse of farm country in the southern part of New Jersey is, and that this marks that area as fundamentally different from the much smaller but very densely populated northeastern area of the state.

In 1935 the four-year curriculum was established and the name of the institution was changed to New Jersey Teachers College at Glassboro. The head was now designated as president, and Dr. Edgar F. Bunce became president in 1937. There was a loosening of restrictions and a revitalized student and faculty participation in the affairs of the institution. Curiously, the enrollment did not reach the high of 1932 until 1939 and then dropped perceptibly during the war. The proportion of men increased during the thirties but, of course, dropped to a handful during the three war years.

The number of male members of the faculty was also increasing. The work load was decreased from a high of thirty-five hours per week in 1923. Tenure was not introduced until 1945.

With the end of the war, as in other colleges, many changes took place. For one thing, a junior-college program was introduced for returning veterans, and this was probably the first step in giving Glassboro a new, general-college coloration, even though it ended in 1949. The presence of veterans also tended to break down the disciplined stance of a predominantly girls' school. Intercollegiate sports became more important. Slowly, the possibility of graduates receiving certification in secondary fields began to open up, and this was to lead to the approval of a graduate program in 1949. While at first the graduate program started with advanced courses for the teaching of handicapped children, for administration of elementary schools, and for advanced work for elementary teachers, it was soon to invade other fields, contributing tangentially to the general college.

Dr. Thomas E. Robinson became president in 1952 and immediately embarked upon a policy of expansion. This policy tied in well with the successful 1951 bond issue for state colleges, which made $2,208,000 available to Glassboro and enabled it to build a demonstration school, a library, a food service and student activity building, and dormitories for both men and women. But curricular changes in state colleges were in the offing, and for Glassboro this meant the right to prepare its students for high-school teaching, which in turn meant the strengthening of liberal-arts departments, bringing Glassboro close to what was to be a major change—its emergence as a general college.

The 1959 college bond issue, which involved both the state university and the state colleges, made another $2,000,000 available to Glassboro and accounted for the following changes. The student center was enlarged and a science-mathematics building was erected—another step in the direction of a general college. A new library and a new gymnasium were built in 1961.

Glassboro was now set for a major increase in enrollment. Secondary-school majors had evolved in social studies, English, music, art, mathematics, science, library science, speech arts, and dramatics. With enlarged possibilities for electives, the symbiosis of teacher-training and liberal arts was almost complete. A new breed of faculty members was brought in, and this, too, helped in the transition The ratio of men to women increased to one third. To cap the climax, Middle States accreditation was achieved in 1958, and in the same year the name was changed to Glassboro State College.

In 1967 President Johnson, seeking a midway point between Washington and the United Nations, selected Glassboro as a meeting place for the summit conference with Premier Kosygin of the Soviet Republic. It was a historic international meeting that seemed a fitting crown to the energetic efforts of Glassboro to become a general college.

In 1963 there was a special report by the committee appointed by Governor Hughes and headed by Dr. Carroll V. Newsom, which called for the transference of all power in higher education to a new State Board of Higher Education. The report also proposed that all state colleges be turned into multipurpose institutions. Dr. Robinson of Glassboro took a leading position with the other state college presidents on the question of having the state colleges remain under the aegis of the State Board of Education. While the State Board of Education seemed to be in the saddle, a report issued by President Goheen of Princeton tilted the balance in favor of the Newsom recommendation. The recommendations were enacted into law on December 5, 1966. It was a new way of life for higher education, but with no group of colleges completely happy. The state university would chafe under the administration of the chancellor who would be heading the Department of Higher Education, the state colleges would be concerned when their budgets were cut, the private colleges would feel that there was too much expansion of public education, creating empty places in their own institutions.

Two new aspects in New Jersey were to affect state college expansion, particularly Glassboro: the 1966 sales tax and the creation of the Educational Facilities Authority. Both released new monies for the state colleges, and Glassboro especially was to benefit from these two sources. A $2,500,000 music building and a $3,500,000 college center were the result of the sales tax. A 500-bed dormitory was approved by the Educational Facilities Authority.

New curricula were introduced and one might say that by the end of the sixties, Glassboro had all the concomitants of a general college—a liberal-arts college. Its faculty was now more oriented toward liberal-arts subjects. Were most of the students still inclined toward teaching? Yes, but that did not diminish its importance as an all-purpose college serving its students and the state. People do not appreciate the fact that subjects in the education major are just as important as other liberal-arts subjects. History of education or educational psychology are just as valid as liberal-arts subjects as a history of wars or general psychology.

Dr. Richard Bjork succeeded Dr. Robinson as acting president for one year, 1968-69, while a search was made for a new president. In 1969 Dr. Mark M. Chamberlain became the fourth president of Glassboro. The Faculty Senate held its first meeting on January 10, 1969. It was an important change from the early administrative pattern when the principal was the ruling authority. Now the Senate had the power to consider any college matter on its own volition. In case of basic disagreement with the president, the Senate had the right to refer the matter to the board of trustees. The power structure had shifted.

Quite apart from the Senate, the faculty was organizing under the banner of the Faculty Association, and in 1970 Glassboro faculty members, en masse, marched with representatives of the other five colleges at the state capital and won their right to be a negotiating body. The main issue at stake was salary. Progress was slow, but now the American Federation of Teachers entered the fray and by a close margin won the vote to represent the six state colleges.

The students, too, wanted a share in the new power structure. Here, too, was a far-reaching change from the closely regimented rules of the early years. Now the students had full responsibilities for their own living regulations, for coeducational living, for the use of alcoholic beverages. They also won the right to have grades sent directly to them, on a pass-no-credit grading system and a number of other matters as well.

The physical growth of Glassboro continued in the meantime unabated. The $6,000,000 music building is probably the best in the state. A $6,000,000 student center is also outstanding, and a $4,500,000 classroom structure and a $2,000,000 dormitory complete the picture. One can no longer say that South Jersey is a neglected part of the state.

William Paterson College

William Paterson College is also a good example of how teacher-training institutions have evolved through the years. It began in 1855 when high-school graduates teaching in the elementary schools of Paterson were given late afternoon and Saturday instruction on how to improve their teaching. Later, day classes were organized, and at this point Paterson became a one-year school for high-school graduates who wanted to go into teaching. In the late 1890s the one-year course was extended to two years. During this period the city of Paterson bore the expense of running the school, but in 1923 the state legislature approved the taking over of the school by the state. From 1923 to 1937 the school was called Paterson Normal School and during that time the course was gradually lengthened to four years, leading to the Bachelor's degree. In 1937 the name was changed to

New Jersey State Teachers College at Paterson. In 1943 two additional majors were added to the curriculum in elementary education: kindergarten-primary education, and its first one in secondary education, the business education curriculum. The latter was transferred to Montclair State College in 1953.

In 1958, the name became Paterson State College, and by 1963 it had expanded its offerings to twelve major programs in elementary and secondary fields.

In 1966 the college began to offer baccalaureate programs in fields other than education, namely, in nursing, English, mathematics, sciences, history, art, and speech. By 1970 four divisions were formed: College of Arts and Sciences, School of Education, School of Fine and Performing Arts, and a School of Nursing. The following year the college moved from Paterson to Wayne, where it had acquired a beautiful new campus. The name was changed to William Paterson College of New Jersey in honor of one of the great leaders of the Revolution era, a Governor of New Jersey and a signer of the Constitution.

Until the move to Wayne the school had only a few rooms, which were gradually increased to eight, in one of the elementary-school buildings. The elementary school itself was the laboratory for the college. But with the move to Wayne, a building campaign took place that was to make the college one of the outstanding campuses in the state.

A word should be inserted about the relationship of the Normal School to the Passaic County Junior College. Elsewhere I recount the story of the emergency junior colleges during the thirties. The Passaic County classes of this college were started in 1933 in the classrooms of the Normal School, and courses were offered in liberal arts, science and engineering, and business administration. When federal money was no longer available, the activities of the junior college were transferred to the State Normal School where they continued until after World War II. In fact, Dr. Robert H. Morrison who, in 1935, was appointed Principal of Paterson State Normal School, also served as supervisor of the emergency junior college program in the state. Thus, the Normal School activities were intertwined with the courses of the emergency junior college, and the Normal School found itself embarked upon a general college path long before formally becoming a general college. Dr. Morrison did everything he could to give the Normal School status as a collegiate institution.

This tradition of general courses was especially important after World War II when many veterans found it possible to receive two years of such courses at the government's expense. It must be stated in passing that twice, in 1933 and in 1938, attempts were made in the name of economy to discontinue the normal school at Paterson. Happily both attempts failed.

Dr. Clair S. Wightman, who succeeded Dr. Morrison, continued the concept of a general college *cum* teachers college and went a step further by establishing an Adult School for the Paterson area in 1938. It might be said that no school building in the United States served as many activities as School #24 in Paterson: demonstration classes, normal school, junior college, and adult center.

One of the distinguishing features, pursued by both Dr. Morrison and Dr. Wightman, was the experience given to students attending the National Camp in Sussex County, and later at the State School of Conservation at Stokes State Forest.

In 1948 Rutgers, the State University, opened an extension at School #24 and for a short period the general courses were dropped by Paterson State Teachers College.

The college opened its new campus in 1951. While the original estate had been purchased by the state, it was through the impetus of the 1951 $15,000,000 bond issue that the college experienced its real thrust forward.

William Paterson, like Kean College, started originally as a city-sponsored teacher-training institution, then became a part of the state system, and later left its very inadequate quarters in an obsolescent part of Paterson and moved into a new community. The outcome was an entirely new college with facilities second to none. However, here again, the teacher-training faculty cannot vanish into thin air even though the college has become a multipurpose institution. Nor do many students want to overlook the advantage of being certified for teaching even though jobs may be scarce in that field. The result is that sixty to seventy percent of the seniors are certified for some level of teaching. After all, it does make sense for a student who is majoring in creative arts or in drama to have a double vocational goal in mind. A college is usually the product of three forces: what the creators, as a rule the board, had in mind, what the faculty vested interests want to impose, and what the students want. This last force is most often a result of the employment situation. William Paterson is a good example of how the three forces operate.

The new campus now has some twenty-seven buildings worth over fifty million dollars. Its new student center is one of the best anywhere and includes a ballroom that can be used for many different types of student functions. The science complex has laboratories of the most sophisticated type. Both a fine arts building and the center for performing arts are also outstanding. A large gymnasium and a modern library are two other impressive buildings, along with a number of classroom units. The coed dormitories, all four-room apartments housing four students each, are probably as commodious as any found elsewhere in the country.

At William Paterson the problem of feeding dormitory students was solved as it has been partly or completely in other colleges, by providing apartment-type dormitories where the students can prepare their own meals. Usually there is a choice of buying and cooking their own foods, or of eating in the college cafeteria. In all colleges, since time immemorial, there has been resistance to institutional feeding, and there were actually food riots or sabotage throughout the centuries. Mass feeding is rarely successful even with the most conscientious attempts to provide appetizing food. But the alternative, that of giving the students the opportunity to cook for themselves, has many disadvantages. One can notice that in many institutions having such an arrangement a number of things happen. A limited number of students, men and women, cook regularly for themselves, and a proportion of these, as a matter of philosophy, eat natural foods only. But by far the largest number tend to cook in a haphazard manner, and their meals are often convenience snacks of low nutritional character. So far I haven't seen such a state dormitory campus that did not have a cake sale going on. Please remember that one reason that led to the eating clubs at Princeton was an attempt to avoid the curse of institutional food. Perhaps the Princeton students had the right idea. If only they had made it more democratic!

William Paterson College illustrates another great plus for New Jersey. Originally the most humble of the state colleges without even an entire building to itself although fulfilling at all times a dedicated and conscientious role as a teacher-training institution, it now has a campus that is one of the best in the state and serves over 8,000 full-time undergraduate students and about 25,000 graduate students.

Jersey City State College

In Jersey City the principal of Grammar School No. 1, George H. Linsley, had established a Saturday Class in 1851 to instruct his teachers. This led to the more formal Saturday Normal School in 1856. The school included some branches of general learning plus principles and methods of education. The older and brighter girls graduating from the public schools were recruited for teaching and given extra training in the Saturday School. In 1872 a high school was established, and at this point the Saturday School was merged with the third year of high school. In 1885, a six-month course, later extended to one year, was started for those high-school graduates who wanted to go into teaching. The Saturday Normal School ended in 1879 because School No. 5, in 1877, had become a practice or training school. In 1886 the Jersey City Training School for Teachers was established. Two departments were included: a model school for observation and a practice school where students could teach under the supervision of critic-teachers.

In 1900 the training school course was lengthened to two years. Courses for teachers such as psychology, history of education, pedagogy, and school management, which had been taught in the high school, were transferred to the training school. But the cost of maintaining this school was becoming a heavy burden upon the city. Besides, under the 1903 state education law, this expense and responsibility was being assumed by the state. Finally, in 1928, $1,215,000 was appropriated by the state for a new plant of what was to be known as the Jersey City State Normal School. The Gothic style of architecture was to be reminiscent of Princeton. It was to be built on ten acres, and this fact is important. Ten acres was deemed a lot of land for a college at that time, but thirty years later by a simple, unnoticed, subjective, and offhand remark of a minor state official, fifty acres became the magic campus size and soon it doubled, tripled and quadrupled. The fact remains that large campuses often defeat the very needs of the institution by making communication more difficult, by encouraging independent empires, by increasing costs unnecessarily, and by making administration more difficult. The only factor that has increased the need for more space is the parking area, but even there a lot of cars can be accommodated in two or three acres.

At any rate, Jersey City was now relieved of an irksome expense and boasted of a beautiful new campus to boot. The school would have two three-year curricula: one in elementary, the other in kindergarten-primary. In 1934 the Bachelor of Science degree was sanctioned by the State Board of Education upon completion of four years of college. It was a far cry from the Saturday morning institutes. In 1936 a five-year course of study was established for the training of school nurses and health teachers in conjunction with the Medical Center. In 1941-42 a two-year general curriculum was approved in business administration, English, mathematics, modern languages, music, science, social studies, and sociology. This might be considered a forerunner of the general college character of the state colleges, which was to come later. This move tended to encourage the placing of liberal-arts courses in the first two years, giving the student an opportunity to think about his professional specialization. During the veteran period there was a further tendency to develop general courses since the veterans could elect them throughout the third and fourth years, completing an arts and sciences program.

In 1962, with the state-financed acquisition of the A. Harry Moore School, the college acquired a laboratory school for the training of teachers for the mentally retarded and physically limited student.

In spite of an outstanding plant, a glorious past of community support, and a vigorous record of accomplishments, there have been occasions when some misguided persons have recommended the closing of the school. This happened twice in the Depression period when there was an oversupply of teachers, and again in 1975 when there was a financial emergency.

11
Two New State Colleges

Ramapo College

IN DISCUSSING Ramapo College one must not forget that the northeastern part of New Jersey, which includes the counties of Bergen, Passaic, Essex, Hudson, and Morris, is the most populated of the state. Essex was well saturated with public institutions located in Newark. The Bergen legislators responded to the public's inclination for a new college by giving them Ramapo, which, as a result of the 1968 $15,000,000 bond issue, was opened in 1971 in Mahwah. The curricular approach here was different from any of the other state colleges. While there were the usual disciplines of liberal-arts colleges, there were established six interdisciplinary schools: American studies, intercultural studies, contemporary arts, theoretical and applied science, metropolitan and community studies, and human environment.

The basic idea was to encourage cross-fertilization among majors and schools. In addition, there are two divisions—teacher education and physical education, and professional institutes. The first is intended mainly for those who wish to teach in the secondary schools and want to combine a major with courses necessary for teacher certification. The latter is intended for those interested in business and accounting careers.

Another aspect of the college includes a tutorial program whereby each faculty member takes care of fifteen to twenty advisees. Students receive two credits for this tutorial work.

Situated in one of the historic and scenic parts of the state, Ramapo has experimented bravely with architectural allocation of space, even to the extent of one-way mirrored walls that reflect the bucolic surroundings.

Ramapo College has embarked upon a courageous new curricular format. It remains to be seen whether the inevitable thrust of discipline-minded faculty, who, after all, are the products of universities that are major-minded, will not ultimately twist the format to suit the all-too-prevalent vested interests that operate in most colleges. The tendencies of faculties are to duplicate what they have been used to and to think in terms of what they do best. Moreover, the natural inclination of students to think in terms of jobs may also bring into greater prominence the teacher-training and the business-administration aspects of the college's offerings. It has been seen how in most, nay all colleges, within the state the hopes, the ideals, the programs of the original founders were lost in the shuffle of events and in the desires of students.

Stockton State College

Once the decision was made on a college in Bergen, the pressure rose for a similar college in the sparse southern area of the state. It was decided to satisfy both areas simultaneously. While these two colleges are included in the listing of state colleges, they really are different in that neither one had the problem of trying to shrug off the image of a teachers college. Both started off as general colleges. But, as it happens in many liberal-arts institutions, the majors begin to take on a vocational cast, and there is nothing wrong with this evolution.

Stockton is in a number of ways sui generis. First, it has 1,800 acres in Pomona—as many as all the other state colleges put together. Second, it represents a major departure from the usual architectural arrangement of the various teaching, administrative, and student units of a college. The buildings are in a snakelike formation connected by a long, wide corridor that in itself serves as a continuous student lounge center. The student dormitories are on the other side of a lake. No professor, no department, no administrative unit "owns" any space. The walls are easily movable. At the end of each academic year changes are made according to the needs of the new academic year. Areas are decreased or increased as needed.

Third, this is a college that started with a bargaining agent already established, since the Federated Teachers Association represents all the state colleges. Under this contract the faculty members are "employees," and it might be pointed out in passing that the imposition of an industrial unionization pattern upon the academic community produces some grey areas. It is not quite certain whether the loss of "collegiality" is totally acceptable to the academic community. There is another aspect to this whole question, and that is the cost of unionization, which includes not only the cost of dues but the cost of institutional time involved in negotiations. The total cost divided by the number of full-time faculty probably diminishes considerably the actual financial benefits of unionization if one accepts the fact that there is a limitation to state or county sub-sidization or to tuition that can be charged whether in public or in private colleges.

Fourth, while this college has one of the largest campuses in the country, it nevertheless does not forget its service to the community and has various off-campus centers where it seeks not only to meet local vocational needs but also to encourage nearby students to embark on a program of general education.

12

Upsala College

UPSALA COLLEGE is another example of the desire of a church group to train ministers for their flock and to educate their members. This time it was the Augustana Lutheran Church, which had founded three colleges in the Midwest. In 1893 it decided to establish a college in the East. The Reverend Lars Herman Beck was chosen as the first president. The college opened that year with an enrollment of sixteen in the Bethlehem Lutheran Church in Brooklyn, New York. The name "Upsala" was selected because that year was the three-hundredth anniversary of the Uppsala decree, which had established the Lutheran Church in Sweden. The college at that time, like many other early colleges, was a combination of a secondary school extending into the first two college years, as was the practice in Europe, and the word *college* had a European connotation. In order to secure a New York State charter, the name had to be changed to Upsala Institute of Learning, for no school with an endowment less than $500,000 could use the name "college." The next year, slightly better quarters were obtained in St. Paul's Church in Brooklyn.

Naturally, the college wanted its own building. Various

locations in Westchester, in Long Island, and in New Jersey were considered. The New Orange Industrial Corporation in New Orange (now Kenilworth), desirous of attracting Swedish-American families to its real estate development, offered a fourteen-acre plot of land. In 1898 Upsala moved to this new location. The entire possessions of the institution were packed into one truck, and the bill for moving was $16.00. While their first building was being erected, the college operated in a rented farmhouse. In 1900 the building was finished and the college moved again. The first floor contained a chapel and classrooms, the second, classrooms, and the third floor, a dormitory where the students lived free of charge. Later on there were more buildings: a girl's dormitory, a commercial hall for the secondary school or academy students who were studying business subjects, and a somewhat primitive gymnasium.

In 1912 the academy and college were definitely separated. Upsala can be given credit for two sensible movements that did not acquire general educational popularity until fifty years later. One was credit without attendance but upon examination. For instance, if a student came in with a knowledge of Swedish, he could be given credit for the course if he passed an examination. The other forward look was credit for correspondence courses.

In 1913 the State Board of Education ratified Upsala's right to give the A.B., B.B., and M.A. degrees. The academy connected with the institution was not cleared for full high-school status until 1915.

Through 1919, out of ninety-seven graduates, two-thirds became ministers while one quarter became teachers.

Kenilworth proved to be an undesirable location, and after examining various sites it was decided to move to East Orange in 1923. At this point, enrollment was about 300. There were three buildings at the start—the Hathaway Mansion and two other houses. Compared to Kenilworth, it was an exhilarating move forward.

The Depression affected the enrollment of the college as it did for most colleges. But after the war Upsala was able to build, and a humanities classroom was dedicated in 1949. A gymnasium was completed in 1956, a library in 1964, and a science building in 1967. A new dormitory for 550 students to augment two smaller dormitories was completed in 1970.

The enrollment has been increasing over the decades until now, leveling off at about 1,200 of whom about half are dormitory students. Upsala is still church-minded, although there has been a shift in synod arrangements for it is now part of the New Jersey-New England Synod, but it receives very little money from the church. The president still must be a Lutheran but is no longer required to be a minister. A goodly part of the faculty is still Swedish Lutheran. There is an emphasis on Scandinavian studies, and a Scandinavian major is offered that enables students to spend two semesters at the University of Stockholm. But only a small segment of the student body is of Swedish Lutheran background. The college draws from all religious and ethnic groups, including almost fourteen percent blacks.

Upsala College is a good example of a small liberal-arts college with career orientation, valiantly serving the communities of New Jersey but also welcoming students from many other states. Its present strength and holdings would have made its brave original founders happy indeed.

Upsala winds up what might be called the colleges that were founded by ethnic-religious communities: Scotch-Irish-Presbyterians at Princeton, Dutch-Dutch Reformed Church at Rutgers, Irish-Catholics at Seton Hall and at St. Peters, German-Presbyterians at Bloomfield, and finally the Swedish-Lutherans at Upsala, although Felician College might be considered a partial Polish-Catholic development. Similarly, the other Catholic colleges for women were involved at the outset mainly with Irish women students. All have lost their national and religious coloration; all are nonsectarian in spirit. Upsala is still slightly tinged with church relations inasmuch as it still receives a miniscule contribution from its synod, but so small an amount as to be practically meaningless.

13

Education for
Catholic Women

IN VIEW of the growing Catholic population of New Jersey during the nineteenth and twentieth centuries, the role of the colleges for women established by various Catholic orders is an important one. One must remember that there was a disinclination in established men's institutions to concern themselves with women's education. The day of coeducation was not to come until many decades later. The energetic approach of the various Catholic women's colleges is therefore all the more remarkable.

In 1889 a college for women named after Sir John Evelyn had been formed near Princeton, and Princeton allowed the girls to use its library, its museum, and even classrooms and laboratories. Professors from Princeton taught some of the classes, which were held in a house about a mile away. By 1897 the enrollment had not exceeded fourteen and the college was closed. This was the first attempt at higher education for women in New Jersey until the College of St. Elizabeth was established in 1899, which became the first permanent college for women in the state, and one of the first Catholic colleges for women in the United States.

College of St. Elizabeth

The College of St. Elizabeth was established by the Sisters of Charity in Florham Park and Madison, and grew out of the activities of the Order in providing for their own novitiates. In the case of Sisters of Charity, their first step outside the training of their own nuns was the formation of an academy or high school, established in 1860.

It is interesting to note the relationship with the Catholic hirerarchy as evinced in the makeup of the board of trustees. The bishop of the diocese is president of the board, while the mother general of the order is chairman. In 1965 the first man was elected to the board and in 1969 five laymen were added.

There had already been courses of post-high-school nature in the academy, roughly equivalent to the first years of college. The organization of a full four-year college course was a natural development upward. The opening of the new building in 1899 synchronized with the first college class of seven freshmen. The College of St. Elizabeth was incorporated in the state of New Jersey in 1900. In 1903, at the first commencement, which was combined with that of the academy, four of these first students graduated.

The main emphasis was on the arts and sciences, but there was early provision for education, secretarial, and household arts courses, although the latter two led only to a certificate. Music was added later.

Through the years practically all the students were boarding students, but during the Depression years of the thirties there was an increased number of day students, and this, too, was a change in the makeup and modes of the student body, since it necessitated a change in the strict rules of the college for boarding students. Eventually, one quarter of the student body commuted to classes. Incidentally, while at the beginning practically all the students were Catholic, in time, fifteen percent were non-Catholic.

At first, practically the entire faculty consisted of sisters. The percentage of outside faculty gradually increased through the years until now perhaps forty percent are lay faculty. As time went on, through herculean efforts and wise use of available funds, important buildings arose. Two dormitories, Santa Rita and O'Connor Halls, were built. St. Joseph's Hall, which houses the gymnasium and swimming pool, the outdoor Greek theater modeled after the one in Ephesus in Greece, Henderson Hall for the Sciences, and Founders Hall, a dormitory built through the Federal Housing Act, are some of the important additions. The Mahoney Library was made possible by the 1963 Federal Education Act.

The College of St. Elizabeth is a good example of an outstanding Catholic college serving not only its own constituency but the general needs of the state.

Felician College

Felician College in Lodi is an example of a bustling Catholic college for girls, established by the Felician Sisters, a congregation based in Krakow, Poland. The Sisters had come to the United States in 1874 to set up a school in Polonia, Wisconsin, to serve the poor Polish immigrants there. In seven years they established schools in other Polish communities in Illinois, Michigan, Indiana, and New York. In 1882 they set up a normal school to train teachers needed in their own schools. They were also supplying other needs, such as an old-age home, an orphanage, and a small hospital. Because of the increasing numbers of Polish immigrants, they were called upon to staff schools connected with Catholic churches in Newark, Jersey City, Camden, Passaic, Trenton, Bayonne, South Amboy, and Perth Amboy. In 1909 or so, it became evident that there was need for a mother house in New Jersey, and it was established on the Hennessy O'Hare estate in Lodi.

In 1923 a normal school was set up to train in-service teachers, qualifying them for state certification. In 1935 this school was raised to the status of a teacher-training college and was affiliated with the Catholic University of America. It was a two-year college whose graduates could go on to complete their degree requirements not only at Catholic University, but also at nearby Seton Hall and Fordham.

Felician College was reorganized as the Immaculate Conception Junior College in 1941. About twenty years later it was empowered to confer the Associate in Arts degree, and in 1964 it began to admit lay women. At about the same time, it took over the three-year nursing program of St. Mary's Hospital in Orange and compressed it into a two-year collegiate program.

In 1967 it took a great step forward. By this time, its physical plant had been developed considerably. It had classrooms, laboratories, a library, and a large and very modern auditorium. The state approved a four-year curriculum. The name of the institution was once more changed to Felician College. It offered four-year programs in liberal-arts and in elementary education.

Felician College has about 700 students in the daytime and is still a women's college. In the evening, in its community program, it does permit men and about twenty-five percent of its evening students are male.

Thus one sees in Felician College the various aspects of the adjustment of what was originally a sister-teacher training purpose to that of a modern college for laymen, expanding its offerings to include men but only in the evening, service-oriented, still church-related, but not a one hundred percent religious faculty, and, generally speaking, opening its doors to the winds of change.

Georgian Court College

Georgian Court College started in what was probably one of the most sumptuous estates in the United States. The Sisters of Mercy bought the estate in 1924 from the estate of Jay Gould, who had built the beautiful setting in 1896. The Sisters had founded Mount Saint Mary's College in 1908 in North Plainfield. Fire destroyed the little college in 1911, but the new building was rebuilt before the first graduation. As the years went by, their growth made it imperative for them to move elsewhere, and it was in Lakewood where the fantastic Gould estate was for sale that they reestablished themselves. It was that great leader of Catholic education in New Jersey, The Most Reverend Thomas J. Walsh, then Bishop of Trenton, and later Archbishop of Newark, who helped them in their move. The curriculum was a strong liberal-arts one, as it is to this very day, but the graduates of the college assume professional tasks in most cases connected with their majors, and teaching, merchandising, science, and law all are represented by Georgian graduates. Interlaced with the liberal-arts core curriculum are sixteen credits in theology.

Caldwell College

Caldwell College was founded by the Dominican Sisters in 1939. They had founded Mount St. Dominic Academy in 1884, and the college step was a natural move upward as it had been for other church-related institutions. The Sisters, as they built Rosary Hall and then Aquinas Hall in 1929, were thinking ahead. Since they were part of the Newark diocese, which included St. Elizabeth's College, they could not get diocesan permission to establish the college until diocesan boundary lines were changed. St. Elizabeth College found itself in the Paterson diocese, leaving the Newark diocese without a Catholic women's college. It was Archbishop Thomas J. Walsh, that prime mover in Catholic higher education, who encouraged Caldwell College to establish itself. Forty-one young women registered for the first class. The curriculum was straight liberal arts with, of course, a strong emphasis on Catholic culture and the philosophy of the great Dominican teachers, St. Thomas Aquinas and St. Albertus Magnus. This did not deter attention to sciences, and indeed many of its graduates found ready employment upon graduation in New Jersey pharmaceutical companies and research laboratories. But teaching was a strong vocational goal, and even secretarial science attracted many students. Music flourished also, both for professional and avocational reasons.

In 1952 the college built a new library. But times change, and Caldwell College, in seeking to serve the community in which it has so long been a part, established in 1969 a coeducational curriculum that functions from 3:45 P.M. to 9:30 P.M. daily, and this, too, was a change in a Catholic college for women.

14

Two Nonsectarian
Independent Colleges

IT HAS been seen how all of the four-year private colleges
have been church-related. Two examples of independent
colleges not connected with any church are Rider and Monmouth. The first represents the evolution from proprietary
business college to a general college. The second has had an
unusual development from public two-year college to independent two-year college to a four-year institution.

Rider College

After the Civil War, with the expansion of commerce in
the United States, there was a growth of business schools,
and this national tendency was exemplified in Trenton at
the dawn of the twentieth century by a number of competing
schools. The Trenton Business College had been affiliated
with the Bryant and Stratton chain, whose aim it was to
have a school in each city having a population of over

10,000. In 1866 Mr. Andrew J. Rider, then of the Newark affiliate, assumed the principalship of the Trenton school. A ladies' department was soon added, although at that time it was not felt that women could assume a place in business. Later, when typewriters were in general use, the first typists were men. Women, at best, might just possibly help out by keeping elementary books. Mr. Rider retired in 1873 to take care of his cranberry interests, but he returned to resume management in 1878. In 1897 the school was incorporated as the Rider Business College. The facilities of the various schools before they coalesced were always rented quarters. Students commuted by railroad or boarded with nearby families.

In 1898 Mr. Franklin Benjamin Moore came into the picture as an instructor and business manager. Within a year he had acquired Mr. Rider's interest in the school.

There was another business school in Trenton, the Stewart and Hammond Business College. It must be remembered that business schools in the United States were then, as they are now, proprietary institutions and generally bore the names of the owners and reflected shifting ownership. In 1886 Stewart became the sole owner and the name was changed to Stewart Business College. In 1901 Stewart became ill and sold his interests to one of his instructors, John E. Gill. After a brief period Mr. Gill merged his school with Mr. Moore's to form the Rider-Moore and Stewart School of Business, although they continued to operate in separate buildings. In 1911 this new school absorbed another business school in Trenton, the Horton-Large Business Institute. In 1913 the school expanded its offerings to include a program of training teachers to teach commercial subjects. Under the "Rider Plan" students could arrange their course of study on an accelerated two-year basis or space it out to four years.

In 1921 the four-story building on East State Street and

Carrol was completed at a cost of about $160,000, and the name was now simplified to Rider College. It had become one of the outstanding business institutes in the country. The following year it acquired college status and was permitted to give the degree of Bachelor of Accounts and Bachelor of Commercial Science.

In 1934 both Mr. Moore and Mr. Gill passed away. Their sons took over: Franklin B. Moore as president, J. Goodner Gill as vice-president. There was no board of trustees as such, but there was a prestigious advisory board. Now began a new phase of the college, for Mr. Moore strove for academic recognition through the Middle States Association of Secondary Schools and Colleges.

A separate library building was completed in 1934 with 16,000 volumes. In 1937 Rider College ceased being a proprietary institution and became nonprofit. A board of trustees of fourteen members was elected forthwith. This was the first step in becoming a true four-year college.

During the war the college suffered a decrease in enrollment, but was able to pull through because of government programs that were awarded to it. As the veterans streamed back, Rider enjoyed its largest enrollment, and immediately thought in terms of expansion.

In 1957 the charter of the college was changed to reflect the desire of the institution to encourage liberal arts in its curricula. That same year, ground was broken for a new campus at Lawrence Township. The first building, the gymnasium, was completed in 1958. By 1964 twenty-seven buildings had been completed including a $1,500,000 library, classroom buildings, dormitories, and a chapel. Liberal arts were now stressed per se in the School of Liberal Arts, and as a concomitant of business curricula. A School of Education and a Graduate School were added at this time. It was now classified as a liberal-arts college, although it had not lost its effectiveness in business curricula, as evinced in its

School of Business Administration. Both sons had well ful-
filled their aims for Rider College. The institution had
served the growing Trenton area, it had weathered staunchly
the problems of the Depression era and the war years, and
it had shown resourcefulness in meeting the challenges of a
postwar period and, finally, in having the courage to strike
out de novo in a new campus and with a new liberal-arts
coloration. It is a good example of a proprietary, then nonprofit college serving the large community within New
Jersey.

Monmouth College

Quite apart from the emergency junior college that existed in the same town, the Highland Manor Junior College,
a proprietary institution located in Tarrytown, New York,
had moved to West Long Branch, New Jersey. Its owner
and president, Dr. Eugene H. Lehman, intrigued with the
Shadow Lawn Mansion, had bought it for $100,000. The
mansion had been built over the site of the former summer
White House by Hubert T. Parson, the president of the
F. W. Woolworth Company. He had spent $9,500,000 to
construct a 128-room mansion on 108 acres in America's
oldest seaside resort area. As the Depression deepened, Mr.
Parsons found difficulty in meeting payments for the taxes
and for the upkeep of the estate. The town finally took it
over for nonpayment of taxes. At any rate, Dr. Lehman
found that supporting this magnificent estate was more difficult than he had envisioned. In the meantime, Monmouth
Junior College was becoming too large for the after-four-
P.M. arrangement with the local high school, Long Branch.
It acquired Shadow Lawn from Dr. Lehman in 1956. Monmouth Junior College, which had started as a quasi-public
emergency college under the supervision of the State De-

partment of Education, had become a private college when federal funding ceased and was now taking over the shell of a proprietary institution. A year later the college was empowered to grant the bachelor's degree. It also started to enroll dormitory students, since there was plenty of room in the mansion. Thus the college acquired a dual character, serving the local commuting students and at the same time receiving dormitory students from an increasingly wide area. It received a 90-acre estate from the Murray and Leonie Guggenheim Foundation and has bought additional surrounding territory. It now also awards master's degrees in business administration, education, electronics, engineering, English, history, mathematics, and physics.

15
Specialized Colleges

Westminster Choir College

NEW JERSEY has been important not only for its church-related colleges, for its liberal-arts institutions, for its engineering institutes, for its teachers colleges now fully evolved into state colleges, and most recently for its community colleges, but it has had and still has important specialized colleges that deserve some mention. One of these is Westminster Choir College. The institution was founded in Dayton, Ohio, in 1926 by John Finley Williamson, an aspiring singer whose career was cut short by a throat infection. He was ably aided by his wife, Shea.

Eventually, the college moved to Ithaca and finally to Princeton in 1932, a move made possible by Mrs. J. Livingston Taylor, who had heard the choir established by Mr. Williamson and gave $350,000 for a new campus.

The institution is interdenominational and has a deep spiritual aspect. There is a sense of discipline and concentration. No drinking or smoking is tolerated. The institution is a combination of a conservatory and a small liberal-arts college. Its majors are music education, choral conducting, performance, and church music. It has no apparent financial worries even though it has less than one million dollars in endowment. It enjoys a 23-acre campus northeast of Princeton. Its students compose a 200-voice choir that gives concerts in major eastern cities and with major symphonies. The students have many weekend responsibilities, usually with churches, and this helps them to meet some of the tuition expenses.

Panzer College of Physical Education

Another specialized institution is the Panzer College of Physical Education, which in 1958 was merged with Montclair State College and, in effect, became its department of physical education.

The Pierson Act of 1917 required that a course in physical education of two and one-half hours weekly be given in all public schools of the state. No normal school within the state was giving courses for the preparation of teachers of physical training and hygiene. Pursuant to the need for such teachers, the Newark Normal School of Physical Education and Hygiene was founded in 1917 with Randall B. Warden and Mathias H. Macherey, director and supervisor respectively of physical education in the public schools of Newark. Classes were held in the rented quarters of the Newark Turn Hall.

There arose, however, the question of conflict of interest, and in 1920 the founders relinquished their interest to Henry Panzer, who then became director. Dr. Margaret C. Brown was brought in as assistant director.

Looking back at its beginnings, Panzer was the only teachers college offering a single curriculum of health, physical education, and recreation. In 1926 Mr. Panzer moved the school to East Orange. Soon three quarters of its graduates were teaching in New Jersey private and public schools.

In 1928 the state approved its four-year curriculum toward the bachelor of physical education. In 1939 the degree was changed to bachelor of science in education. The college enjoyed an enrollment of about 200 students and reached its full stature as a specialized college, with half of its courses of a liberal-arts nature, in 1932 under the presidency of Dr. Margaret C. Brown who had been dean since 1921.

The 1958 absorption of the college by Montclair State College was a logical development, since Montclair had established its own curriculum in physical education, which was competitive with Panzer. Panzer ceased to exist as an independent institution. Thereafter, the Montclair courses in physical education, health professions, and recreation were administered by the Panzer School Council, and the building that contained the gymnasia, swimming pool, classrooms, and laboratories was constructed on the Montclair campus and was named the Panzer School Center.

The Institute for Advanced Study

The Institute for Advanced Study is sui generis. It is really a community of scholars who are gathered together in Princeton, each to continue the study and research in his field. In some ways it resembles a university or a research institute except that there are no scheduled classes involved and no degrees are conferred. There is no commitment that all branches of learning be represented among its faculty. The institute is devoted to learning, and each member is therefore encouraged to continue his education and to expand his contributions in the field. No pressures are put upon him and he may do his work in whatever manner he wishes.

It was founded in 1930 by a gift from Mr. Louis Bamberger and his sister, Mrs. Felix Fuld. A board of trustees of fifteen members was created who in turn would elect a director. The first director was Dr. Abraham Flexner, and he was succeeded in 1939 by Dr. Frank Aydelotte. Dr. Robert Oppenheimer followed in 1947, Dr. Carl Kaysen in 1966, and Dr. Harry Woolf in 1976.

At the present time there are four schools: mathematics, historical studies, natural sciences, and social science. There are no laboratories and no experimental programs. Not all academic disciplines are represented. The students are really the visiting members, and all of them have already received their highest degree.

In the founders' letter, the course of the institute was defined as follows: "The primary purpose is the pursuit of advanced learning and exploration in fields of pure science and high scholarship to the utmost degree that the facilities of the institution and the ability of the faculty and students will permit." At first the professors were all in pure mathematics and mathematical physics. A little later, appointments were made in archaeology, historical studies, and economics. Relatively recently, a modest beginning has been made in social sciences with the appointment of three professors. Funds have come in from foundations and a few corporate sources. There are 26 professors in all and 150 members, about half of whom are invited by the faculty, with the others selected from the many applicants. About half of the members are supported by grants-in-aid from funds available to the institute; the other members are supported by their own universities, by the United States, by foreign governments, and by private foundations. About one third of the scholars come from Europe and Asia; the most famous was, of course, Albert Einstein.

The institute exists in symbiosis with Princeton University, which implies close academic and intellectual relations, but no administrative ties. This also means that the university library is available to faculty and members.

The institute buildings house a small library, restaurant, common rooms, offices for faculty and members, seminar, and lecture rooms. A housing project is also operated for temporary members.

16

Fairleigh Dickinson University

by Clayton Hoagland

THE UNUSUAL CHARACTER of the institution that became Fairleigh Dickinson University was conceived in the midst of the great Depression of the 1930s. It became a living reality in the middle of World War II when it opened in Rutherford, New Jersey, as a junior college. Its extraordinary growth and spreading influence have been without precedent in American higher education.

The college thrived and developed its strength and stability at a time when an intense national drive for reconversion from a wartime climate produced a raw "reconfusion" in some areas of American life. As it expanded, Fairleigh Dickinson's policies and principles were skillfully tailored to fulfill the needs of an area that felt the population outburst and the commercial-industrial growth of the postwar years. Distinctive in its clear-cut aims and innovations, the junior college that opened in 1942 promptly earned the interest of the region's educators. It attracted much local cooperation.

A direct ancestor was Columbia University's New College, an experimental unit founded in 1932. A primary principle of this New York venture was to merge individual scholarship with a range of experiences. These comprised in part some foreign experience, living abroad, an understanding of rural living conditions in America, and personal involvement in community affairs. During the founding years of New College one of the active spirits who joined its faculty was Dr. Peter Sammartino, who taught Romance languages and wrote textbooks for students of French.

A son of immigrant parents, Peter Sammartino had worked for degrees from the College of the City of New York and, with a doctorate from New York University, had studied at the University of Paris. He had married Sylvia Scaramelli of Rutherford, New Jeresy, who had been graduated from Smith College and obtained her masters at Columbia. Her father, Louis Scaramelli, an importer, shared Dr. Sammartino's enthusiasm for the idea of launching a small two-year college that might realize some of the ideals and aims of New College. He succeeded in arousing the interest of Colonel Fairleigh S. Dickinson who, with Maxwell Becton, headed a rapidly growing firm that produced medical instruments in a plant in East Rutherford.

Colonel Dickinson directed one of his executives, Edward T. T. Williams, to investigate the prospects of realizing such an idea as that proposed. Dr. Sammartino soon enlisted the high-school principals in a dozen communities in Bergen and Passaic counties. Their response confirmed his belief that a college with something of the vision and experimental ideals of New College was needed. Professional surveys of that New Jersey area disclosed an abundance of favorable conditions—a soil in which such a venture could certainly take root.

The initial financing by Mr. Scaramelli and Dr. Sammartino, with matching funds from Colonel Dickinson, totalled

$60,000. The state, in 1942, approved incorporation of the college. The board of trustees comprised not only the president, Sammartino, his father-in-law, and two executives of the Becton, Dickinson Company, but also the supervising principal of Rutherford's schools, Dr. Guy Hilleboe. The abandoned building chosen for the founding was held for taxes by the local bank, of which Colonel Dickinson was a director. It could be bought for $21,500. This odd-towered structure of brownstone had once been a family mansion built in the 1880s on a fenced tract of eight acres by David Ivison, a textbook publisher. Locally it was known as Iviswold or Ivison Castle. For a period it had been used by service clubs for luncheon meetings. After years of neglect its conversion for the needs of a college required many months of hard labor. In this the Sammartinos were continuously and physically involved.

The first catalog of courses went out in the spring of 1942. The new junior college was dedicated on September 12. Mrs. Sammartino volunteered as Dean of Admissions. The title gives no adequate suggestion of her active part in the college's founding and growth. Over the years ahead she would become of incalculable importance in all aspects of Fairleigh Dickinson's development.

The first freshman class of sixty students were all girls but one, and there were ninety evening students enrolled. A few years later, the college received full accreditation from the Middle States Association of Colleges.

Behind this modest façade was a force of astonishing power. The potentials of the college were centered on the spirit, the faith, and the drive of Peter Sammartino. Concealed by the serene, thoughtful personality was a genius for swift, direct action and accomplishment. This was to startle the educational world far beyond New Jersey in the years following the opening of the junior college.

Henry Thoreau believed that our lives are frittered

away by detail. "Simplify the problem of life," he wrote, "distinguish the necessary and the real." Dr. Sammartino had a talent for reducing difficult problems, and he recognized it in the colleagues whom he attracted for the heavy work ahead. He gave his trustworthy members among administrators and faculty the freedom to make decisions, knowing that all of them would not be the right ones. "The best we can do," he would say, "is to act intelligently on the basis of the facts at hand."

As president he believed also that the strongest generating force could grow from sound educational purposes: to provide a vital, dynamic cultural background, and programs of training in the liberal arts, business, and the medical arts. Courses in science and engineering were added in 1943-44. Fraternities and sororities were banned on the campus, and at the start college sports restricted. Encouraged were personal sports such as golf and tennis that graduates could use later in life. However, when the new gymnasium was opened for use in 1959, a full schedule of sports, beginning with basketball, came with it. Today, Fairleigh Dickinson teams are nationally ranked in soccer, baseball, basketball, cross country, wrestling, and indoor track. Only football is missing from the schedule.

One of the important pioneering directions was Dr. Sammartino's promotion of more active interest in international affairs. He not only worked to encourage foreign students to enroll, but set up courses in the history and problems of such changing areas as the Middle East, Asia, and Africa. He also arranged for studies abroad by members of the faculty, in the social sciences and other departments, and for an increasing number of seniors.

By 1945 a Board of Industrial Advisors had been formed to enlist northern New Jersey's business enterprises for teamwork in devising curricula. Hearty cooperation of the whole region's high schools was assured from the start.

Thus were the girders of a remarkable structure firmly based.

The final season as a junior college came in the winter of 1947-48. Enrollment by then exceeded 1,100, of whom 632 were full-time day students. The annual budget had swelled to $306,000, and the first formal fund-raising campaign was under way. By November of 1951 the Middle States Association of Colleges had accredited Fairleigh Dickinson as a four-year college. A year later the first dormitories were opened in Rutherford.

An essential force in the growth was a constant interest and active cooperation drawn from a diversity of elements with varied viewpoints. Not only were local high school principals serving on the college's Board of Educational Directors, but the viewpoint of the students was continually polled, and their critical aid repeatedly invited. Many bold advances in education can be slowed to a shuffle by the shackles of precedent, but Fairleigh Dickinson seems to have made experimental thrusts more easily than some older, well-endowed institutions. Its innovations took hold.

A new and dramatic stage of growth came with the development of a campus in Teaneck, nine miles northeast of Rutherford. There, Bergen Junior College on the shores of the Hackensack River had been opened in 1933, and during the first few postwar years enrollment had spurted to almost 1,500. But lack of accreditation by the Middle States Association led to sharp declines. Its buildings were woefully inadequate, and the faculty uncertain of the future. The merger with Fairleigh Dickinson College was announced in 1953. Further physical growth came in stages as Fairleigh Dickinson added acreage along the Hackensack's shores.

More important in its long-range significance, this merger opened new roads for an unexpected, vital expansion of all the plans and policies of the eleven-year-old institution. Before this growth could be efficiently directed, however, the groundwork had to be laid by very hard work. Members of the Rutherford faculty pitched in to prepare the long-neglected equipment and buildings of the Bergen College plant for immediate practical use. This difficult and voluntary labor meant everything to the educational services of Teaneck campus.

In the decade that followed the new pattern of multiple campuses shaped the entire future of the college. Not only was the total faculty increased and improved, but an impressive series of modern buildings was begun along the Hackensack's shore. By this time the original Rutherford campus was strained to the bursting point with more than 1,200 day students and nearly 1,800 evening students. It had become the state's third largest college.

From the beginning the Teaneck campus helped to solve problems, but new ones had been inherited, or created. In the acquired buildings no maintenance had been done for about five years. New curricula had to be devised, as well as an overhauled and expanded program of student activities.

In Rutherford a moderate but promising advance into graduate education in evening programs was made in the fall of 1954. Business management, accounting, and new courses in economics and sciences were added. Other additions were made as graduate enrollment gradually climbed. New classroom buildings were put up, and a gymnasium and a laboratory. A handsome library was opened, named for Dr. Allen Messler, the teacher-scholar who had aided in many ways the early development of the junior college.

Fairleigh Dickinson attained university status in 1956 when it was fourteen years old, with the full approval of the State Board of Education. In that year it also opened in Teaneck the first dental school ever established in New Jersey. In the remodeling of the university's structure, four distinct undergraduate colleges emerged, for liberal arts, science and engineering, education, and business administration.

A third campus, which opened new directions in growth that had been beyond the administration's hopes until then, was acquired in the summer of 1957. This was the magnificent estate of the Twombly family, a tract of some 160 acres in Madison and Florham Park near Morristown, New Jersey. Mrs. Twombly was the granddaughter of Cornelius Vanderbilt. In the grounds of her home stood a mansion of a hundred rooms, a luxurious carriage house, and a recreation building with swimming pool and indoor tennis court. The estate that became available for purchase offered buildings that could be converted to classrooms, dormitories, offices, and a research laboratory.

These Florham Park-Madison facilities soon provided for a full range of liberal-arts courses and new programs in science and in business, with an evening division that drew hundreds of students from a growing and wealthy area of the state.

To assure more smoothly integrated planning for the university, an Administrative Council was set up in 1957. This was virtually a presidential cabinet consisting of the officers and the deans. It made possible closer teamwork with the various faculty committees and Dr. Sammartino's Advisory Committee. From the beginning the president had striven to encourage the participation of young people in all major plans of the college, and thus of the university.

By the twentieth anniversary of its founding, 1962, the faculty in all campuses numbered 360 full-time and almost 600 part-time members. During the early years of that decade of the sixties, enrollment ranged narrowly from 18,000 to 20,000 students. The problems of management for such a widespread operation were reduced by bringing them under the supervision of a University Council. With

76 members, this body came to be known as the University Senate, deriving its authority from the board of trustees. It made possible an extensive participation of the faculty in plans and decisions.

A bold and commendable experiment was set in motion in the spring of 1964 with the dedication of Edward Williams College. This handsome structure built on the shore of the Hackensack River opposite the Teaneck campus is a two-year college with about 400 students. Its innovative programs include liberal-arts studies, with some training for social leadership. Its purpose is to provide a firm educational base for those students who, on graduation, transfer to the university.

A year after the opening of this junior college the university acquired a former U.S. Army missile base of twenty-seven acres in Wayne, New Jersey, some twenty miles southwest of Teaneck. This is under the direction of the Rutherford campus, and buildings on the site were converted to classrooms, a library, and an office. Its programs and facilities are focused on serving those who could not meet college admission standards, and in both day and evening courses it provides important preparation for about 800 students.

In 1967 Senator Fairleigh Dickinson, the son of Colonel Dickinson, gave to the university a site of eight acres in St. Croix, Virgin Islands. In June of 1967 a modern marine biology laboratory was opened on this site. The step was typical of the promptness with which a venturesome private university can often move to keep abreast of the frontiers in such an expanding field as the natural sciences.

The university set up an honors program in May 1967, a program that got off to a good start with thirty-two hand-picked scholars enrolled for individual studies in both graduate and undergraduate courses. Both as an incentive and as an efficient means of strengthening exceptional talent and aptitudes, this soon proved to be a fruitful addition to the university's policies.

An extension overseas came in June of 1965 with the dedication of the university's Wroxton College, twenty-five miles from Oxford. This historic estate had been an abbey remodeled and occupied in 1618 by Sir William Pope on property of nearly sixty acres. Much later, under George III, it became the home of the prime minister, Lord North. Fairleigh Dickinson assigned the task of supervising Wroxton's programs to Dr. Loyd Haberly, a former Rhodes Scholar who had been a versatile and popular dean on all three of the New Jersey campuses. Wroxton has provided undergraduate education from September until May, and attractive summer sessions for graduate students, which draw enrollment from all over the United States.

Dr. Sammartino in the fall of 1965 announced his retirement as president, with the approach of his quarter-century observance, as soon as replacement was feasible. He cited the growth of heavy responsibilities and a desire to cut his working hours to about fifty a week.

He was appointed chancellor, and the board of trustees arranged for dedication of the Peter Sammartino College of Education at the end of 1966. At these ceremonies he and Mrs. Sammartino received honorary degrees of Doctor of Laws. Both of them had been productively active in many remarkable ways during the quarter century since the founding of the junior college in the castle in Rutherford. They were acclaimed for their faithful labors in what had become a unique educational achievement.

Dr. J. Osborn Fuller, a former dean of the College of Arts and Sciences of Ohio State University, became president in October 1967. On his resignation six years later he was succeeded by Dr. Jerome Pollack, who had been, in fact, the active head of the university for the preceding one and one-half years.

Important expansion has continued. On the Teaneck campus the Joseph L. Muscarelle Building for which Mr. Muscarelle has made a gift of $1,400,000 because of his friendship with Dr. Sammartino, will be maintained for a series of courses under the general head Curriculum on Building Construction.

As of 1976, Fairleigh Dickinson University is the second largest college in the state, with an enrollment just under 20,000. This is an astonishing growth from that first freshman class of 60 students in the day and 90 evening students in 1942.

17
Two-Year Colleges

VARIOUS two-year colleges have been established within the state throughout the years. In 1918, spurred on by Dr. David B. Corson, superintendent of schools, Newark Junior College was founded by the Newark Board of Education as an evening college using the South Side High School building. It was very successful, considering the difficulties under which it operated. In 1922, however, Newark felt that it could not afford $175,000 for a separate building, and as a result the college closed.

Rider and Centenary started two-year institutions, and their stories are related in other chapters. Two private law schools, one in Camden, the other in Jersey City, opened two-year feeder colleges for their law schools, the first in 1927, the other, the following year. Bergen County Junior College, which started in the Bergen YMCA in Hackensack and then moved to a campus in Teaneck in the late thirties, had a checkered career until it was absorbed by Fairleigh Dickinson University in 1954.

In 1933, at the height of the Depression, a junior college using a high-school building in Roselle in the evening, was initiated and organized by Dr. Arthur L. Johnson, then county superintendent of schools in Union County. There were 243 students and 14 instructors involved in this embryonic experiment. Soon there were 5 such emergency colleges established: Essex County at the State Teachers College in Newark, Middlesex County at Perth Amboy High School, Monmouth County at Long Branch High School, Morris County at Morristown High School, and Passaic County at the State Normal School in Paterson.

The college at Monmouth started in 1933 in the Long Branch Senior High School building and was open each school day after 4:00 P.M. This followed the same pattern that operated in California during the first and second decades of the century, when, through the efforts of State Senator Anthony Caminetti, junior colleges were established for after-school hours in various high schools in the state. In a period when few went on to college, the idea was to make it possible for those who could not afford to go away to college to have at least the first two years. It was thought at the time that the taxes on the few oil wells for the new-fangled invention called the automobile might help to support this inexpensive and minimal program. The taxes rolled in in ever-increasing waves, and this late-afternoon plan blossomed forth into plush community college buildings that served the adults of the community as well as the young people.

In New Jersey, during the Depression, the motivation was somewhat different. For one thing, establishing these colleges created jobs for unemployed college teachers. It also took young people off the job market, and kept them busy and out of trouble. Out of the six colleges that were created, only two survived after the federal funding ceased—Monmouth at Long Branch and Union at Cranford.

While the motivation at that time was of an emergency character, there was a broader philosophy proposing a statewide system of junior colleges that would coordinate with existing institutions. This ideal was not reached until 1962 when the community-college movement succeeded in New Jersey on a solid financial and educational basis.

In 1936 the federal money ran out, and Passaic and Essex closed, Morris and Middlesex lingered on, but in turn were forced to close during World War II. Monmouth and Union both became private institutions.

But there were a number of other experiments with two-year institutions. Most of them were organized in order to provide education and training for religious personnel. Immaculate Conception Junior College (now Felician College) opened in Lodi in 1941. Villa Walsh Junior College was established in Morristown in 1948 and Assumption Junior College in Mendham in 1952. Others were Archangel College in Englewood Cliffs in 1952, which became Englewood Cliffs College but then closed its campus, which later became the Bergen County campus of St. Peter's College in 1975. Tombrook Junior College in West Paterson was established in 1956. Mount St. Mary College of North Plainfield reactivated its 1905 collegiate charter and became a two-year institution in 1965, but discontinued its program in 1970. Salesian College opened in North Haleden in 1957 and Alphonsus College in Woodcliffe started late in 1968. As was the case in church-related colleges since the beginnings of our country, there was a dual nature to these colleges: that of training the workers for the church involved, and that of bringing in outside students. The two goals did not always mesh, and usually when the outside students either petered out or were discontinued, there weren't enough religious students left to warrant a full-fledged college even though it was only a two-year one. Four two-year colleges for men desiring to train for the priesthood were formed between 1947 and 1956, and the last ceased to exist in 1970. Two church-oriented two-year colleges emerged as general colleges: Northeastern Collegiate Bible Institute at Essex Fells, and Alma White College at Zarapath. Later these institutions became four-year colleges. Conversely, some four-year colleges established two-year divisions. In 1939 Jersey City State Teachers College, experiencing decreasing enrollment, established a two-year general-education curriculum. That same year, Newark College of Engineering (now the New Jersey Institute of Technology) opened a junior division.

Toward the end of World War II, in order to take care of returning veterans, Bayonne and Jersey City established two-year colleges. Glassboro and Newark State Teachers College opened two-year units, and Rutgers established off-campus centers at Atlantic City, Englewood, Morristown, Trenton, and West New York in 1946. In 1947 the Trenton School of Fine and Industrial Arts was upgraded into a junior college. All of these units were discontinued when the veteran rush subsided except Trenton, which became a part of the newly established Mercer County Community College under the 1962 County College Act.

Union, having started as a federally financed institution using the Abraham Clark High School in Roselle during the evening, became a private institution in 1936, changing its name to Union Junior College. In 1942 the college moved to Cranford after buying the Grant School and became a day college. Its main purpose was to serve as a liberal-arts transfer junior college. In 1947 it changed its name to Union College, although it was still a two-year school. After the 1962 act became a reality, a Union County Coordinating Agency for Higher Education was set up in 1965, and it was made a part of the Union County Agency that now had two campuses—one, the upgraded county vocational school, and the other, the general education campus of Union College. By special act of the legislature, money was funneled to the county, which then apportioned it to the two campuses. Thus, Union College, having started as a public college, reverted to the public designation after having existed for twenty-six years as a private college.

Independent Two-Year Colleges

Assumption College

The Assumption College for Sisters in Mendham, New Jersey, which proposes to give a humanistic preparation to future teachers and nurses, is a good example of a small, church-related college that seeks to prepare its students for a technological culture. It is a sister-formation college conducted by the Sisters of Christian Charity.

The earliest beginnings were in 1927 when the Mallincrodt Novitiate School was formed. In 1932 a new motherhouse was erected. Additions were made in 1941, 1951, and 1956. In 1952 Assumption Junior College was founded as a separate entity. In 1960 it was given the right to confer the Associate of Arts degree and that year changed its name to Assumption College for Sisters. It still shares its beautiful campus of 112 acres with the motherhouse of the founding order. A six-credit course in theology and one in philosophy, out of sixty-six credits, is about the only religious commitment required by the college. Students go on to a third and fourth year heavily weighted sister-formation or may transfer to a different four-year institution. Since the attraction for sister-formation is diminishing, the college admits students from other sister congregations and even those who desire a Christian education but have not made up their mind on entering the order. It now has about thirty-two students, all sisters.

Centenary

One college that illustrates how an institution may change over the years is Centenary College for Women. The original decision to found the institution was made at the Newark Conference of the Methodist Church in Washington, New Jersey, in 1866. To celebrate the 100th anniversary of the Methodist Episcopal Church in America the name "Centenary Collegiate Institute" was decided upon and a charter was granted by the state in 1867. Various towns vied for the privilege of being chosen as the site for the proposed seminary, but ten citizens in Hackettstown secured the location by pledging ten acres of land and $10,000 in cash.

The Reverend George H. Whitney was chosen as principal of the school, which at this point was really a co-educational preparatory school and a senior college for women. The building, which was to cost about $100,000, was completed in time for the opening in 1874. There were 108 boarding students, plus a number of day students. Their ages ranged from 10 to 32. All but 6 were Methodists. There was a department for young ladies that was a regularly chartered college empowered to award the degree of Mistress of Liberal Arts or Mistress of English Literature.

The year was divided into three terms: two of thirteen weeks and one of fourteen weeks. The music department was the largest one in the school. At the first commencement in 1876 there were twelve ladies who received degrees from the Ladies' College and sixteen young men who had completed the college preparatory course.

Apparently, Centenary was the first college in New Jersey to have an extension, for in 1896 the president, Dr. Wilbert P. Ferguson, established an evening branch of C.C.I.'s commercial department in Washington, New Jersey. In the

1896-97 catalog, strangely, there was no mention of the Ladies' College, and apparently it had been decided to discontinue it.

On October 11, 1899, there was a fire and the whole building burned down. To meet the contingency, Centenary became temporarily a day school, meeting in a rented hall. In 1901 a new building arose, and, literally, Centenary was reborn out of the ashes of the old school. At this point, a subpreparatory department was established. Centenary was a secondary school emphasizing college preparatory courses: classical, Latin scientific, and scientific. Its building valued at $200,000 was considered to be "the best equipped school in Methodism" and was entirely free of debt by 1902.

In 1910 it was definitely decided to make the institution one for girls only, and in the words of its president, "a young Ladies Female Seminary for Feminine Girls." The boys played their last baseball game and left in sadness. But in the years 1913-18, a post-high-school division gradually emerged with two years of college work. As this phase developed, the subacademic part of the institution disappeared. By 1929 the college years were formally coalesced in a junior college that in 1932 was duly accredited by the Middle State Association of Colleges and Secondary Schools.

In general, a preparatory school was supposed to be a feeder for the college, but at Centenary this was not happening, and so in 1936 the first two years of the high school were dropped and in 1940 the entire preparatory school ceased to exist. Centenary was now Centenary Junior College. In 1956 the name was changed again to Centenary College for Women. It was during this decade that the College's charter was amended and the institution became to all intents and purposes an independent, nonsectarian one. It was to reach its highest enrollment in 1970 with 666 registered students, which dropped to 483 in 1975. But under the presidency of Edward W. Seay, who was to ad-

minister the college for twenty-eight years, longer than anyone else, still another change was to occur—the adding of
the junior and senior years with a Bachelor of Arts degree
given in four areas: general studies, performing arts, medical technology, and early childhood education. About one-
eighth of the student body responded to this new extension
of the junior-college years. In a way it was a return to the
original four-year ladies' college, although the areas of
study reflected the new emancipation of women.

Edward Williams College

Edward Williams College in Hackensack, while a part of
Fairleigh Dickinson University, falls into the category of
an independent two-year college. It started in 1964 as an
experimental college, the idea being that a small college
limited to about 400 students would give greater service
and have a more integrated operation. The college has its
own separate building, which includes a library. Aesthetically,
and this too was part of the experiment, the idea was to
avoid the stereotyped classroom atmosphere: practically
every room different, wall-to-wall carpeting, a small auditorium so that all the students could gather for weekly
conferences and lectures. There was maximum emphasis on
out-of-class activities: symphony, opera, theater, ballet,
sociological visits. The curriculum was uniform liberal arts
consisting of English and literature, psychology, contemporary society and economics.

Students could take one elective at the university across
the river, and make minor substitutions for good reasons.
At the time, the plan was to break up the university into
colleges containing the first two years followed by a three-
year college leading directly to the master's degree. Leonard

Dreyfuss College was thus established in Madison as the three-year complement.

The experiment created an institution where every faculty member knew every student and where every student knew every other student. Guidance was easy and unobtrusive. Reading habits were carefully nurtured and all in all Edward Williams was a good antidote for the massive, impersonal educational complexes where often the student is lost in the shuffle.

Luther College

In 1919 a group of Lutheran pastors and laymen organized the Lutheran Bible Institute in St. Paul, Minnesota. Ten years later the college moved to Minneapolis where it grew and developed. After World War II three satellite colleges, stemming from the main institution, were established—in Los Angeles, in Seattle, and in New York City. The New York School, founded in 1948, occupied quarters in the Gustavus Adolphus Lutheran Church in Manhattan until 1951 when it moved to Teaneck, New Jersey, and was known as the Lutheran Bible Institute. It has grown steadily and now has seven buildings on an eight-acre campus.

At the outset the curriculum was largely theological, but in the early 1960s liberal-arts courses were added and the college changed the name to Lutheran Collegiate Bible Institute. In 1967 there was another change of name, this time to Luther College of the Bible and Liberal Arts.

In the beginning the major thrust was to train leaders for the Lutheran Church activities, but the aim of the institution has now broadened, the basic emphasis being the development of Christian foundations of living in the world of today and tomorrow. Its aims include: "appreciation of God as revealed in Christ Jesus," "commitment to Christian standards of conduct," "commitment to service as a way of life," and "ability to use the Bible." While two-fifths of its students are Lutherans, there are nine other religions represented and almost one-sixth are Catholic.

Some students may prefer this alternative type of education, this attachment to service ideals. In this case, this is a two-year institution and graduates can transfer for the third year to scores of accredited colleges in the United States. There is an advantage in attending a small institution. At Luther College there are about 124 students, half of whom are boarding students. The spiritual ideals that guide the faculty and students may be a good antidote to mass secular education.

18
Community Colleges

OF ALL the educational developments in New Jersey, that of the community colleges has probably been the most dramatic. It has been seen how public colleges in New Jersey go back to the thirties, when during the Depression year, in order to provide jobs for unemployed teachers and, what is usually not mentioned, in order to keep unemployed youths off the streets, the Federal Emergency Relief Administration was established. Then came an era of private junior colleges, and during the early forties there was even a New Jersey Junior College Association that was later absorbed in the newly formed New Jersey Association of Colleges and Universities.

During the fifties, in examining the various alternatives for meeting the needs of college spaces in the state, it became evident that public two-year colleges should have a decided role. But rather than having the state set up such a system, it was decided that the formation of such community colleges would be left to the county, with the state contributing $200 per full-time equivalent or one-third of the cost, whichever was less. Later, the $200 figure was raised to $600. Within five years, six such colleges were established in the counties of Atlantic, Camden, Cumberland, Mercer, Middlesex, and Ocean.

In 1968 and 1969 eight more community colleges were established in Bergen, Monmouth, Burlington, Essex, Gloucester, Morris, Somerset, and Union. In the latter county an agreement was reached whereby the existing private two-year college, Union College, together with the newly established Union County Technical Institute, would function as the community college for the county. This was an interesting example of how a private institution would be saved from extinction by merging with a new public one. Finally, community colleges were opened in Passaic (1971) and in Salem (1972). Thus, sixteen colleges were opened in a period of six years, a most notable achievement. In addition there is the Hudson County College Commission, which will be explained later. It has been shown in the first chapter how far ahead of New York City New Jersey is.

By 1975 the cumulative full-time equivalent in county colleges had risen to about 70,000. But the importance is not the numbers alone. The community college made it possible for masses of disadvantaged students, practically all black or of Spanish surnames, to attend college. By 1973 these minority groups had reached almost nineteen percent of the entire enrollment. Certain colleges have attracted a greater percentage than others, notably Essex, Passaic, and Atlantic, and to a lesser extent, Camden, Hudson, and Mercer. Quite apart from the minority question, these community colleges were making it possible for young people of low-income, and even many of middle-income families to attend college. It is this factor that to a great extent helped to bring down the percentage of New Jersey students going out of the state from fifty-four to forty-five. In all of the community colleges students may take a two-year sequence that would be the equivalent of the traditional liberal-arts pattern and then transfer to the third year of a four-year college. The state colleges have been especially cooperative in encouraging this upward movement.

The second important development is that because of the open enrollment policy, the natural tendency of having public education continue after graduation from high school has been greatly reinforced. It's not exactly free education since there is a tuition fee of about $400 a year, but there are a number of programs that make it possible for even this low tuition to be absorbed. In other words, in this country, but particularly in New Jersey, any student who is motivated is assured of two years of college beyond high school.

A third factor that is outstanding is the breadth of vocational curricula that serve the needs of the communities. With the increasing complexity of our technological advance, there are thousands of jobs available in the semiprofessional fields, and it is this need that the community colleges are filling to an admirable degree.

Fourth, this widespread movement, which is national in scope, makes for a more commonsense approach to higher education. It seems to the author more rational to break up higher education into the first two years, to be followed by those who wish to continue by three more years, leading directly to the Master's degree. The preponderant growth of the two-year college movement and its especial development in New Jersey emphasizes this measured cadence. One of the purposes of the two-year college movement is to give the student an opportunity to adjust to college, to think out his educational and occupational life style, and to lessen the chances of failure and frustration.

Fifth, because of their evening and adult programs, the community colleges are adding to the sum total of services to the communities involved. From the educational and job-advancement perspective, this has importance. From the sociological point of view there is an even greater advantage. True, the state university, the state colleges, and the private colleges were already doing a great deal of this. But now, the state and the counties have added a whole new panoply of offerings.

Sixth, almost all of these county colleges have started off with sparkling new campuses, all of which are now in a sense community centers, and this, too, adds to the total cultural splendor of the state. As of 1976, a total of $251,454,735 has been authorized for these centers. For a small state this is not an inconsiderable sum. All of these institutions have adult and cultural activities. In the past, colleges were built slowly, starting with humble buildings, adding facilities as meager resources permitted. But the community colleges in New Jersey were practically created overnight, with striking architectural design, adding considerably to the beauty of the countryside.

Each of the colleges except one started with all the concomitants of a good educational plant: sufficient good classrooms, laboratories, library, gymnasium, cafeteria, and student recreational hall. All except the Passaic County College were started on a spacious campus. In the case of Passaic, the idea was to have the college in an urban setting in order to help stabilize the Paterson area. It lacked the full complement of facilities for a while, but now it has the full adjuncts of a good institution. Essex County College, while not enjoying the immense acres of the others, has an outstanding plant on acreage that would be considered generous for any urban institution and on a par with any of the other institutions in the Newark complex for higher education. It, too, acts as a stabilizing force for the inner city. On the other hand, Mercer, Camden, and Atlantic elected to move away from the crowded cities, building where there was more space.

Some of the colleges, notably Passaic County Community College and Brookdale Community College, bravely experi-

mented with different types of teaching, using specially prepared materials and cassettes, teaching on an independent
basis. In the case of Passaic, it was decided to return to
traditional teaching methods primarily because the students
were not responding to unorthodox type of instruction,
which requires maturity and great personal responsibility.
There is another problem still to be settled. What rights on
copyrighting such material does the teacher have? Textbooks have been evolved within schools and the copyright
claimed by the instructor while he was being paid by the
school. Does the same hold true for a series of slides or for
movies or cassettes?

Of the sixteen colleges, Middlesex, Morris, Mercer,
Brookdale, and Bergen have the largest enrollments, in that
order, and all have over 6,000 students. The small ones are
Salem and Passaic, both under a thousand. What is more
important is that in five counties that had neither public nor
private institutions, each now has a two-year community
college. In Mercer, Trenton Junior College and Salem
County Technical Institute were precursors, respectively, of
the present community colleges. The community college has
also changed the educational aspect of the southern part of
New Jersey, which is no longer the neglected part of the
state. It now has seven county colleges: Burlington, Ocean,
Camden, Gloucester, Salem, Cumberland, and Atlantic.

Four counties, because of a low-population base, do not
have two-year colleges: Cape May, Hunterdon, Sussex, and
Warren. They may send their students to other community
colleges through a "chargeback" mechanism. Minority per-
centages of enrollment vary greatly. In Essex, which is in
Newark, it is 68%; in Atlantic, 34%. It is lowest in Morris,
3%, and in Bergen, 2.6%. The average is about 19%.

From a vocational perspective, business, law enforcement,
and nursing are by far the most popular courses offered.
While it is true that only about one-fifth of the total full-

time enrollment finally graduate, it is equally true that five-sixths of the graduates go on to further education. Another aspect that is important is that this phalanx of sixteen new colleges represents a distinct "eager beaver" approach, and this is all to the good. Too often in education the tone is hardened by the long-standing, tenured professors who resist change.

The original formula was $200 each by state, county, and student This was gradually abandoned, and now the state contributes about forty percent, and the county and students share the remainder.

All in all, the community-college movement has been the most significant step forward in the history of higher education in New Jersey, and it has been accomplished faster than any similar movement in any state.

The community colleges are county-based institutions with autonomous boards of trustees but subject to policies and regulations of the State Board of Higher Education.

In Hudson County a different type of community college developed. Curiously, after the war, Jersey City had started a junior college that functioned in Dickinson High School after the regular secondary-school classes were over. The expenses were minimal since the tuition for the students was paid by the Veterans Administration. When the veteran period was over, the need for such a college disappeared, and although there were some civilians who would have used a two-year college facility, Jersey City did have a state college and St. Peter's College. Besides, the finances of the city were such as to discourage the assumption of any new endeavor in higher education. In fact, the county did not feel it could embark upon a community-college enterprise either, even though the cost would have been roughly only one-third of the total expense of such an institution. Instead, Hudson County Community College Commission was created and a compact was entered into with three institutions:

Jersey City State College, St. Peter's College, and Stevens Institute of Technology. Students could, with proper guidance, take courses at any of the three institutions and receive their associate's degree from the institution they attended. The commission also has centers in five other towns where courses are given. Financially, the commission operates in the same fashion as the other community colleges and receives its share of help from the state.

The state support of community colleges amounted to $37,280,000 in 1976, with the county commitment about $45,000,000 more. The total budget, which includes student tuition, is about $115,000,000. There are about an equal number of students divided between career courses and liberal arts.

19
Medical Education

FOR MANY YEARS New Jersey did not have a medical school. Then, in 1960, Seton Hall University under the leadership of Monsignor John L. McNulty decided to establish one in the Jersey City Medical Center, which had been founded by Mayor Frank Hague. The famed political leader was born on a kitchen table and his mother died in childbirth. As he achieved power he swore that some day he would build a hospital for the people and that it would be one of the best hospitals in America. And he tried to do just that when he created the Jersey City Medical Center, mostly with WPA labor. As time went on, after his death, the hospital began to have financial difficulties, and in order to cut down expenses and bring in extra income, the directors invited Rutgers University, Seton Hall University, and Fairleigh Dickinson University to consider using facilities at the Center for a medical school. It was Monsignor McNulty who saw the opportunity he had long cherished and accepted the challenge. He was right in his basic thinking. At the Jersey City Medical Center, classroom and laboratory space was ample, the clinical material was available, and medical research could be developed. There would be no dearth of applicants. The tuition would cover the classroom cost of full-time instruction both in the two-year preclinical period and in the last two years of clinical instruction. There would have to be many part-time adjunct professors who would take care of special courses, but in most cases these would contribute their services. The research activities would have to be covered by grants.

There were two developments by the time the institution got to the clinical years. The hospital doctors who headed the different departments were not ready to give over the control to the university's professors. Also, the expenses rose far beyond what had been expected, principally because of the greater number of full-time professors required by the American Medical Association accreditation procedures. The result was that in 1965 Seton Hall decided to sell its medical school to the state for $4,000,000.

Rutgers University, in the meantime, had started a two-year medical school at Piscataway near New Brunswick in 1962. It could not succeed in getting the state to give the money for a full-fledged four-year operation and had to content itself with the first two years of preclinical subjects, the students transferring for the third year to established medical colleges.

The state, incidentally, had decided to transfer the former Seton Hall school to Newark, placing it near the existing Martland Hospital. Newark was retrogressing and needed a prestigious medical school in its midst.

Finally, since both Rutgers and the Newark operation, now baptised as the New Jersey College of Medicine and Dentistry, were financed by the state, Governor Cahill in 1970 felt it would be better if both operated under one administration under the Board of Higher Education in Trenton. The college now has almost 500 students in medicine in Newark plus almost 200 students in dentistry. The Piscataway campus, now elevated to four-year status, has about 300 students. There are in addition 60 students in graduate research. There is what is called the Fifth Channel, a special one-year program for graduates of foreign medical schools in order to integrate them into interneships and residencies in New Jersey hospitals.

The question arises—why is it that seventy-five percent of the resident physicians in New Jersey hospitals are graduates of foreign medical schools? The answer would seem to be that medical education is still research and specialty oriented. Furthermore, the American Medical Association, through its various accrediting procedures, does not particularly encourage a breakthrough in getting more general practitioners, especially in isolated communities. There has been a movement to produce more internists, more family-practice men, more pediatricians. But the process is slow and all in the name of necessity of upholding higher standards. In the meantime, about seventy percent of the general-practice physicians in New Jersey are graduates of foreign medical schools, which, on the average, do not come up to American standards.

The Newark operation spreads over a forty-six-acre area, and $189,000,000 has been spent so far for a galaxy of six gleaming white buildings, including a new one for Martland Hospital.

Since the state budget was undergoing some trying experiences, the school decided to raise tuition from $1,750 to a more realistic figure, the rationale being that loans could be extended to those who couldn't pay and that these loans could be easily repaid upon graduation when the income of new doctors might be $40,000 a year.

The name of the entire school is College of Medicine and Dentistry of New Jersey and includes the New Jersey Medical School, the New Jersey Dental School, the Graduate School of Biomedical Sciences, and the Rutgers Medical

School. It also includes a community mental-health center, two hospitals for clinical practice, Martland Hospital in Newark, and Raritan Valley Hospital in Greenbrook, which unfortunately contains only 131 beds, not enough for the clinical needs of the Rutgers school. There is a yearly budget of $90,000,000, half of which is provided by the state.

20
Thomas A. Edison College

ONE of the most imaginative educational services that New Jersey renders to its citizens is through the Thomas A. Edison College, established in 1972. This college is a mechanism that enables students of all ages to acquire a degree, even though they have not matriculated at an established college. There are many persons, young and old, who, either because of a new pattern of living or because they have shied away from the intricacies of registering for a college course, simply have not followed through with a college education. Thomas A. Edison College gives them a new opportunity. It does not in itself give any courses, but it does award associate and baccalaureate degrees.

Its services include both an evaluation of any courses the applicant may have had and guidance for future study toward a degree. In other words, it is a state college for external degrees. It will seek to interpolate into college credits any knowledge or experience of college grade. It seeks to encourage any motivated individual to proceed with his college education and to simplify the mechanical transference of credits that often discourages a student. Those who receive the Associate in Arts degree can continue in any of the state colleges, and probably in any other public or private institution for that matter. Psychologically, it can be a great help to the older or retired person who hesitates to attempt to continue or embark upon a college career.

There are four ways in which students may meet degree requirements: previously earned college credits, proficiency examinations, service-school attainments, and individual attainments. Individual assessment of college-level knowledge may be through experience, through independent study, or sometimes through study at nonaccredited institutions. In other words, the college seeks to evaluate such knowledge that has been gained in nontraditional ways.

The college gives its own examination in a number of subjects. It also grants credits for examinations given under the College Level Examination Program as well as the Advanced Placement program of the College Entrance Examination Board. It also interpolates into college credit, courses and examinations given by the United States Armed Forces Institute. Finally, it has six counseling centers around the state to make it easier for prospective students to receive guidance.

Its fees are minimal: twenty-five dollars for enrollment and usually twenty-five dollars to fifty dollars for subject examinations, so that cost need not deter students. All in all, it is a tremendous service to the citizens of the state, and it is another example of how New Jersey is in the vanguard of higher education in the country. Having said this, it should be pointed out that most private colleges within the state, as well as the State University, also have mechanisms for evaluating other courses or other experiences in order to facilitate a student's continuance in higher education. Sometimes, vested interests and academic hypocrisy prevent a full transference, but the rigidity of the past has given way to a more rational assessment of meeting requirements for a degree, often circumventing the meaningless, time-serving elements that for a long time have had a stranglehold in higher education.

21
The Changing Scene

IN ASSAYING what has happened in New Jersey, one must remember that generally when one talks about what a state is doing for higher education, what is really meant is what is it doing for *public* higher education. Naturally, during the eighteenth and nineteenth centuries, the problem of higher education had been met mostly by church-related private institutions, and these were mostly in the East. As America developed in the Midwest and the West, there were fewer of these church-related colleges in those states, and the need for higher education was met by state appropriations. Therefore, on the record, if one examined what various states were doing for higher education (meaning public higher education), there was apt to be, ostensibly, a better record in the Midwest and West. Since in certain states in the East the need had been met by private colleges, there was for a time a disinclination to expand public higher education too fast. A further retardant was the depression decade, followed by the war years, and the few years beyond them when very little of a creative nature could be done because of the chaotic veteran readjustment period.

The mid-century mark becomes a fairly good point from which to observe the immense changes in higher education following the war. The G.I. Bill undoubtedly emphasized the government's participation in democratizing post-high-school education, although all of the major movements to be described would probably have taken place even if the bill had not been enacted. There is no question that in Washington the mood was set for major help to higher education —in buildings, in certain tuition payments, in research. In New Jersey, as in all other states, this meant an enormous infusion of federal money.

But New Jersey, like most states, also changed its attitude. Let me reiterate that during the thirties there was little money. In many cases budgets were reduced. There was a Spartan attitude prevailing. But once the readjustment to peace had been completed, there was a different feeling. Young people had been inured to the general concept of post-high-school education for all or almost all. The concept of institutional debt far into the future was easily accepted. The idea of luxury for all pervaded the college campuses. Where before a simple student commons met the needs of the undergraduates, now student unions became larger, more commodious, even in some cases having poolrooms and ballrooms. Gymnasium buildings had to include Olympic-size pools, saunas, rooms for special indoor sports. Theaters had to have the full perquisites of the advanced professional stages. Huge parking facilities were necessitated by new modes of travel.

Where before a private institution counted on a capital expense of $4,000 to $5,000 per student and disregarded part-time students in its computation, now the figure was apt to be ten times as much, computed on a full-time equivalent basis, which is an entirely different thing. Where before capital expenses were met from contributions, from student tuition, or from bank loans, now were added various federal

ABSTRACT

and state sources, in some cases loans, in others, grants, matching or outright, and in still others, like the 1963 Federal Higher Education Law, a combination of grants and loans. Gone was the penny-pinching attitude of yester-year. Architects and campus-planning experts vied to make bigger, better, and more dazzling campus complexes. The debt service mounted each year—federal, state, county, and institutional. In a way it paralleled what was happening to the American family, which had changed from a cash basis to a perpetual debt basis and where the debt service was really a part of the operational expenses. Certainly in private institutions this had become so, and the tuition had to be adjusted to include these payments.

Rutgers, the State University, went through a complete metamorphosis, and there was a major change in the state attitude, in expansion of service, in the profusion of build-ings, in enrollment increases, in new campuses. The state colleges went through two adjustments, one in the expansion of campuses, very different from their former cozy layouts, and second, when they became general colleges. The com-munity colleges hit the state with the greatest impact since the founding of the nation—sixteen new campuses, practi-cally all architect's dreams. The whole concept of what higher education offered by the state should be was changed.

Also, the differences between public and private colleges and universities were blurring, no matter what proponents of one or the other would have the public believe. For one thing, Rutgers had really changed over from partly private to public. Was the institution any different? No. Was the faculty of a different breed? No. Were the cars the students drove better or worse? No. Were the curricula different? No—except that now there was money to add new courses. Were the members of the board of trustees a different type of people? No. Boiled down to the one essential difference, it was simply that in one case the state was subdizing a far greater share of the capital and operational expenses. But even when it comes to private institutions the state and the federal government were subdizing them to some extent. New Jersey, for instance, donates about $6,000,000 from its take in the lottery to private institutions; it makes equal opportunity grants to them; it gives scholarships to meritorious students in private institutions.

Other modifications are in process. The rise of nonsectarian private institutions, such as Fairleigh Dickinson University, Rider, and Monmouth, is one, whereas before private institutions were always church-related. But even among the private institutions there was a crossing of lines between church-related and nonsectarian. One can say definitely that during the last thirty years or so there has been a desecularization of the church-related colleges. Also, church-related colleges no longer limit themselves to members of their own faith. Fairleigh Dickinson University has more Catholics than Seton Hall, which, incidentally, used a student wearing the Star of David in an advertisement. The caption was, "You don't have to be Catholic to attend Seton Hall." And Upsala, originally Swedish and Lutheran, has far more black students than Bergen Community College. This secularization takes place for two reasons: there is a disinclination on the part of students, not so much with girls but certainly with men, to attend institutions on the basis of strict religious conformation, and second, the requirements of federal and state laws prevent appropriating money for the propagation of any specific faith.

Throughout, also, is the lessening of emphasis on straight liberal-arts or straight humanities programs and a sliding emphasis toward career programs, even by colleges that make a virtue of their liberal-arts stance. In the community-college field it works the other way, but for different reasons: to keep open the possibilities of transferring to senior colleges and probably because of the influence of accrediting associations, which tend to stress general education at the expense of too narrow a vocational training. And, of course, it has been shown how the teachers colleges became general colleges, which means emphasizing liberal arts. But even at general colleges, the students are career minded and tend to follow those courses which lead to jobs. On the whole, one might say that a homogenizing process has been going on and that all colleges tend to follow more or less the same mold.

I have shown the phasing out of two-year independent institutions for a number of reasons. First, two-year colleges became four-year colleges. Second, a number of the two-year schools were limited to girls and combined religious training with liberal arts; today there are fewer women attracted by religious vocations. Besides, most girls like to go on to coeducational institutions. Last, the public community colleges offer stiff competition, and the only way for a two-year Union College to survive was to become a public college.

But it was also the end of an era for the four-year private or independent college. One indication is that there have been no new four-year institutions, although a few two-year institutions have expanded to four years. But from now on there probably will be no new two- or four-year independent colleges. Also, the proportion of private college students in the overall state enrollment has been steadily decreasing until now it is a bare twenty-two percent, and even this percentage will decrease, especially since the public institutions use the full-time-equivalent statistical method. In one case, the difficulty of a private college has led to bankruptcy, although the institution is taking on new life and promises well.

But while church-related institutions are going through a process of desecularization, two new theological colleges have been formed, both Jewish, and this, too, represents a change in ethnic representations.

The doors have been opening for minority groups and for low-income families, and this is an important development. But the record is not always the same. In Newark (except for the state college), in Camden, and in Jersey City the colleges have remained to help retain and build the bastions of the city. But the state colleges in Newark and in Paterson found it convenient to move out,—an academic version of the flight to the suburbs.

The centralization under the Board of Higher Education has been a major development with no segment completely happy. The State University feels that it should not be subject to a central body. The state colleges feel that they should get more. The independent colleges feel that they are more or less ignored. Everybody wants maximum subsidization and appropriation with minimal control. Finally, with the faculty, the adoption of unionization has changed the character of one of the oldest professions. The professor had a certain aura about him—some call it *collegiality*. Now, according to state contracts, he is an employee just like the factory worker. Administration is equivalent to management. The chairman is squeezed in by both.

Note that all of these changes are paralleled in most other states, but they represent a shifting development in the state of New Jersey. The important thing to remember is that whether one speaks of the splendor of buildings, of the dedication of faculty, of the panoply of curricula, or of the variety of research, New Jersey is in the forefront.

Bibliography

Books

Bole, Robert D. *More Than Cold Stone. A History of Glassboro State College 1923–1973*. Glassboro, N. J.: Glassboro State College Press, 1973.

Brower, Walter Ashley, Jr. *The First One Hundred Years*. Trenton, N. J.: Rider College, 1965.

Brown, J. Douglas. *The Liberal University*. New York: McGraw-Hill, 1969.

Burr, Nelson R. *Education in New Jersey 1630–1871*. Princeton, N. J.: Princeton University Press, 1942.

Cunningham, John T. *University in the Forest: The Story of Drew University*. Florham Park, N. J.: Afton Publishing Company, 1972.

Custard, Leila Roberta. *Through Golden Years 1867–1943, A History of Centenary Published for the Seventy-Fifth Anniversary*. New York: Lewis Historical Publishing Company, Inc., 1974.

Jarrold, Rachel M., and Fromm, Glenn E. *Time the Great Teacher*. Princeton, N.J.: Princeton University Press, 1955.

Keller, Reverend J. William. *The Centennial Story of Seton Hall University 1865–1956*. South Orange, N.J.: Seton Hall University, 1956.

Kennelly, Edward F. *A Historical Study of Seton Hall College*. Ann Arbor, Mich.: Zerox University Microfilms, 1975.

Lengyel, Emil, and Mackensen, Heinz F. *The First Quarter Cen-*

tury: A History of Fairleigh Dickinson University, 1942–1967. South Brunswick and New York: A. S. Barnes, 1974.

Lynch, James M., Jr. *Born of Necessity.* Vineland, N. J.: Standard Publishing Company, 1970.

McCormick, Richard P. *Rutgers: A Bicentennial History.* New Brunswick, N. J.: Rutgers University Press, 1966.

McEniry, Sister Blanche Marie. *Three Score and Ten: A History of the College of St. Elizabeth 1899–1969.* Convent Station, N.J.: College of St. Elizabeth, 1969.

Murray, David. *History of Education in New Jersey.* 1899. Reprint. Middle Atlantic States Historical Publications, no. 12. Port Washington, N.Y.: Kennikat Press, 1972.

Rudolph, Frederick. *The American College and University.* New York: Alfred A. Knopf, 1968.

Sammartino, Peter, and Rudy, Willis, eds. *The Private Urban University, A Colloquium.* Rutherford, N.J.: Fairleigh Dickinson University Press, 1966.

Sammartino, Peter. *Of Castles and Colleges.* South Brunswick and New York: A. S. Barnes, 1972.

Schmidt, George P. *Princeton and Rutgers—the Two Colonial Colleges of New Jersey.* Princeton, N.J.: D. Van Nostrand, 1964.

Taylor, Harry T. *Bloomfield College: The First Century, 1868–1968.* Bloomfield, N.J.: Bloomfield College, 1970.

Wertenbaker, Thomas Jefferson. *Princeton 1746–1896.* Princeton, N.J.: Princeton University Press, 1946.

White, Kenneth B. *Paterson State College—A History 1855–1966.* Paterson, N.J.: Student Government Cooperative Association of Paterson State College, 1967.

Reports and Papers

Bowen, William G. "Princeton University—Report of the President." Princeton, N.J.: Princeton University, January 1974.

Brown, J. Douglas. "The Paradox of Princeton" (Remarks Made at the President's Conference with Alumni Leaders, October 5, 1974). The Alumni Council, Box 291, Princeton University, Princeton, N.J.

————. "The Personality of Princeton" (Address to the National Alumni Association, February 23, 1967). Princeton, N.J.: Princeton University Press, 1967.

Bruins, Elton J. "The New Brunswick Theological Seminary, 1884–1959." Ph.D. dissertation, New Brunswick Theological Seminary, 1962.

Calman, Alvin R. "Upsala College in Kenilworth." Manuscript. East Orange, N.J., 1976.

Cunningham, John T. "New Jersey Colleges" (series of 27 weekly articles). *Newark Sunday News,* November 1955–May 1956.

Davis, Earl C. "The Origins and Development of New Jersey State Teachers College of Montclair." Ph.D. dissertation, New York University School of Education, 1954.

"Federal Support to Universities, Colleges and Selected Nonprofit Institutions, Fiscal Year 1973." A Report to the President and the Congress. Washington, D.C.: National Science Foundation Surveys of Science Resources Series, 1974.

Fishler, Bennett H., and Zuccarello, Anthony (Chairman and Vice-Chairman, Council of County Colleges). "New Jersey Community Colleges—The First Ten Years 1963–1973." A Report of the New Jersey County (Community) Colleges to the State Legislature. Office of Community College Programs, 225 West State Street, Trenton, N.J. February 1975.

Fjellman, Carl. "Upsala College, 1893–1968." Manuscript. East Orange, N.J.: Upsala College, 1968.

Kirschner, William L., Jr., Chairman. "Annual Report" (New Jersey Educational Facilities Authority). 1974.

League of Women Voters of New Jersey. "Higher Education in New Jersey." Edited by Mary Fairbanks. Montclair, N.J., 1960.

Leonard, Janet Grandy. "History of the Curriculum of Newark State College 1855–1934." Manuscript. New Brunswick, N.J.: Rutgers University, 1971.

Lilien, David, Chairman. "University College—A College at the Turning Point." New Brunswick, N.J.: Prepared by a Committee on the Problems and Prospects of University College, Rutgers University, 1929.

McKeefery, William J. "The William Paterson College of New

Jersey Annual Reports 1973–74." William Paterson College, Wayne, N.J.

O'Donnell, James. "Jesuit College in Jersey City." Jersey City, N.J.: St. Peter's College, 1972.

Sherman, John. "The Origin and Development of Jersey City State College, 1927–1962." Ph.D. dissertation, Jersey City State College, 1969.

"Sketch of the rise, progress, and present state of the Theological Seminary of the Presbyterian Church in the U.S." Elizabeth Town, N.J.: Shepard Kottock, 1817.

"Teacher Education for a Changing World." Montclair, N.J.: Montclair State College, 1958.

Wacker, Hazel M. "The History of Panzer College of Physical Education and Health 1917–1958." East Orange, N.J., 1959.

Index